Music Therapy
Reimbursement:
Best Practices and Procedures

Music Therapy Reimbursement:
Best Practices and Procedures

Judy Simpson, MHP, MT-BC

Director of Government Relations
American Music Therapy Association

Debra S. Burns, PhD, FAMI, MT-BC

Postdoctoral Fellow
Indiana University School of Nursing

The American Music Therapy Association, Inc.

Published by the
The American Music Therapy Association, Inc.
8455 Colesville Road
Suite 1000
Silver Spring, MD 20910

Tel: (301) 589-3300
Fax: (301) 589-5175
Email: info@musictherapy.org
Website: www.musictherapy.org

ISBN: 1-884914-13-6
Printed in The United States of America

Neither the American Music Therapy Association, Inc. nor its Executive Board is responsible for the conclusions reached or the opinions expressed in this publication.

DISCLAIMER
Nothing in this document is intended to imply a guarantee of reimbursement success. This publication is designed to serve as a guide to music therapists and others in the reimbursement process. Music therapists should refer to the guidelines, rules, and/or regulations of their individual facilities, institutions, localities, states, the AMTA Standards of Practice, the AMTA Code of Ethics, and any other applicable governing laws and regulations.

Contents

CONTENTS, cont.

Acknowledgments

The wealth of information contained in the three existing association publications on reimbursement was the starting point for this new guide. Some of the same techniques and tools from these resources have been included within this new publication with appropriate updates to reflect current practice. I would like to express my thanks to the many individuals who contributed to the development of these earlier reimbursement guides.

The Reimbursement Guide for Music Therapists: Phase One (1990)
Co-edited by Mary Scovel and Becki Houghton

The Reimbursement Primer (1998)
Developed by members of the AMTA Reimbursement Task Force and
National Office Staff, Erica Jarvis and Angela Jeter

The Reimbursement Primer Supplement (2001)
Developed by Mary Helen Ekstam and Amy Reynolds

Many thanks to the Mid-Atlantic Region of AMTA Executive Board and the following AMTA members under the leadership of Mary E. Boyle, Ed.D., MT-BC for generously contributing the annotated bibliographies of music therapy research, originally prepared for the National Institutes of Health "Music and Medicine Symposium" on March 20, 2003.

Michael D. Cassity, Ph.D., MT-BC   Russell E. Hilliard, Ph.D., LCSW, MT-BC
Anne Lipe, Ph.D., MT-BC   Paul Nolan, M.C.A.T., MT-BC, LPC
Edward A. Roth, M.M., NMT, MT-BC   Jayne M. Standley, Ph.D., MT-BC

Special thanks to Debra A. Burns, Ph.D., FAMI, MT-BC, co-author, for her assistance with this publication over the last two years. From designing the web-based survey, to compiling data and authoring the best practices section, Deb was instrumental in seeing this project through to completion.

To the therapists who responded to the surveys, emails, and phone interviews, thank you for your willingness to share your successes and your challenges to benefit the profession, the association, and the clients our members serve.

To members of the AMTA Executive Board, thank you for your leadership in recognizing the need for the reimbursement initiative.

And finally, to my co-workers in the AMTA National Office, and to our Executive Director, Dr. Andrea Farbman, thank you for your unending support and encouragement in making this publication a reality.

Introduction

This publication is a tangible outcome of the American Music Therapy Association's (AMTA) Strategic Plan Reimbursement Priority, first established in 2000. In its continuing efforts to further the association mission of advancing public knowledge of music therapy benefits and increasing access to quality music therapy services, the AMTA Executive Board selected reimbursement as the first strategic priority and then developed an operational plan initiative. Over the last two years, several tasks have been completed that are designed to address the plan's Reimbursement and Financing Primary Goal:

Increase access to music therapy services by increasing the percentage of music therapy services receiving reimbursement.

In preparing this guide, a review of previous music therapy reimbursement publications was completed. The progress the profession has made in some areas regarding reimbursement is significant. More music therapists are seeking third-party coverage and more music therapy services are receiving payment from those reimbursement sources. The recognition of music therapy has increased tremendously since the publication of *Reimbursement Guide for Music Therapists: Phase One* in 1990. The historic "Forever Young: Music and Aging" Hearing before the United States Senate Special Committee on Aging in August 1991 was instrumental in increasing awareness and access to music therapy. Because the hearing's success resulted in legislative advances, demonstration projects were funded through the Older Americans Act, which ultimately led to the inclusion of music therapy as a reimbursable service under Medicare's partial hospitalization program.

In other areas, the progress has not been as easy to measure due to tightening state and federal budgets and the rising cost of healthcare and health insurance. At the time of publication (January 2004), the United States Congress has just completed one of the longest debates concerning Medicare reform. Healthcare issues and costs currently top the agenda of many business executives' meetings and almost all union contract negotiations. Recognizing the logistical challenges that continue to exist, AMTA has more advocacy work ahead in order to achieve the goal of increased reimbursement. It is encouraging, however, to acknowledge our accomplishments thus far, and know that we are on the right road, following the path that was paved by our peers in related therapy professions.

As the healthcare environment becomes more complex each year, it's important to stay abreast of the changes in healthcare financing. The tools needed to succeed in today's market are much more diverse, requiring as much attention to the business of music therapy, as to the clinical applications of music therapy. This guide is designed to address today's business needs through three main sections. First, it provides the basics—healthcare financing 101, explaining current methods of payment for healthcare services and outlining the process of seeking reimbursement for music therapy. Second, it presents best practice examples of music therapy reimbursement, based upon results of interviews conducted with AMTA members during 2003. Third, this guide provides sample forms and marketing materials essential to the reimbursement process.

Music Therapy Reimbursement Basics

Reimbursement and Financing of Music Therapy

In responding to calls from AMTA members and music therapy consumers, one area of confusion that often arises is the difference between reimbursement and financing of music therapy services. Traditionally, the term *reimbursement* suggests third-party reimbursement or third-party payment. A third-party payer is defined as:

> an entity, such as an insurance company, that has agreed via a contract (that is, the insurance policy) to pay for medical care provided to the patient. "Third-party" refers to the involvement of another entity besides the two parties directly involved in medical care, the patient and the physician. Third-party payer is frequently used interchangeably with insurance company, insurer, or payer. (Blount & Waters, 2001, p. 290)

Third-party payers include federal programs such as Medicare and TRICARE, federal and state programs such as Medicaid, state programs funded through departments that oversee health issues, and private insurance companies.

Financing of music therapy services can involve different mechanisms for payment which are not as narrowly defined as insurance reimbursement. Typically, when discussing "financing of music therapy," the payer is not as directly involved in the process. For example, grants that pay for music therapy services do not involve a contract for each individual client served, as is required for insurance reimbursement. Usually grant funding is allocated as a dollar amount, often given for specific program areas so that music therapy services can be provided for an identified client population, such as a hospice program. The grant money is not earmarked per client based upon a benefit policy, but instead the distribution of funds is determined by the actual grant proposal. As such, grants are not considered "reimbursement."

Another example of financing for music therapy is payment for school-based special education services, which are included on a child's Individual Education Plan (IEP). Music therapy is considered a related service under special education law, currently titled, Individuals with Disabilities Education Act (IDEA).

When a music therapy assessment demonstrates that the service is necessary for a child to benefit from his/her special education program, music therapy services must be included on the child's IEP and paid for by the school district. Funds for related services are received by the school district from the state, which receives a percentage of funding from the federal government. It is the decision of the school district to determine how best to utilize the special education funding received. So, similar to the grant concept, a lump sum is distributed throughout the district based upon student and program needs. Even though funding comes from the state and federal governments, it is not considered traditional third-party reimbursement due to the method of distribution.

It is important not to get too concerned about whether or not you are seeking "reimbursement" or "financing," as the ultimate goal is to increase access by obtaining funding for the services clients need. It is important, however, to be educated on the different terminology that is used in funding healthcare services so that you can be successful in this environment.

Reimbursement Sources

Medicare

Medicare is the federal health insurance program for people age 65 and older, people under age 65 with certain disabilities, and people with End-Stage Renal Disease (permanent kidney failure requiring dialysis or a kidney transplant). It is divided into two parts, Medicare Part A, Hospital Insurance and Medicare Part B, Supplementary Medical Insurance. Part A provides coverage for inpatient care in hospitals (including mental health care) and skilled nursing facilities (not custodial or long-term care). It also helps cover hospice care and some home health care provided the client meets certain conditions. Most individuals with Medicare Part A do not pay a monthly premium because these expenses are paid through employment Medicare taxes.

Medicare Part B assists with coverage of physician services, outpatient hospital care, durable medical equipment, outpatient mental health care, and laboratory services. Individuals who elect to have Medicare Part B pay a monthly premium and enrollment is voluntary. Part B also covers some physical and occupational therapy and some home health care that Part A does not cover. Medicare Part B provides for services and supplies when they are medically necessary. The Centers for Medicare and Medicaid Services (CMS) define medically necessary as services or supplies that:

- are proper and needed for the diagnosis or treatment of [a] medical condition,
- are provided for the diagnosis, direct care, and treatment of [a] medical condition,
- meet the standards of good medical practice in the local area, and
- are not mainly for the convenience of the [patient and the provider].

(United States Department of Health and Human Services, 2003, p. 74)

The Centers for Medicare and Medicaid Services (CMS), formerly the Health Care Financing Administration (HCFA), is the federal agency responsible for the management of the Medicare program. CMS is part of the U.S. Department of Health and Human Services (HHS) which includes the Administration on Aging (AoA), Centers for Disease Control and Prevention (CDC), Food and Drug Administration (FDA), the National Institutes of Health (NIH), and several other agencies. Within CMS, there are 10 regional offices throughout the country, which provide customer service, oversight of operations, evaluation of programs, and education and outreach to beneficiaries and providers. (Centers for Medicare and Medicaid Services, *Medicare Information Resource,* 2003).

All Medicare payments are processed through fiscal intermediaries (FI). FIs are usually insurance companies that serve as financial agents for CMS. These companies process claims and issue payments on behalf of government programs or other insurance organizations. In other words, CMS headquarters, based in Baltimore, Maryland, does not process Medicare claims. CMS interprets regulations and provides guidance on the implementation of the Medicare and Medicaid programs. CMS then contracts with insurance companies to administer the programs. The terms *fiscal agent* and *third-party administrator* are sometimes used to describe FIs.

Medicare Reform

Following months of debate and negotiation, the United States Congress recently passed the Medicare Prescription Drug Improvement and Modernization Act of 2003. President Bush signed the bill into law on December 8, 2003. This legislation is the most significant change to the Medicare program since it was established in 1965. Along with other provisions, it adds coverage for prescription drugs, expands coverage of preventive benefits, increases fee for service payments for physicians and rural providers, and creates the Medicare Advantage program, which incorporates private health insurance plans. Implementation of the law's provisions is scheduled throughout 2004, 2005, and 2006. To stay current with changes occurring in the Medicare program, please visit the CMS website: www.cms.hhs.gov

Music Therapy and Medicare

Since 1995, music therapy services have been eligible for Medicare coverage when provided as part of a partial hospitalization program (PHP). The requirements for successful reimbursement include that the treatment be considered "active." Active treatment mandates that the service be supervised and evaluated by a physician, be reasonable and necessary for the treatment of the individual's illness or injury, and be goal directed and based on a documented treatment plan. In addition, there needs to be a reasonable expectation that the client will improve with the intervention, not simply maintain current level of function (Centers for Medicare and Medicaid Services, *Medicare Benefit Policy Manual,* 2003).

All services submitted to Medicare for payment must include an established code that describes the presented procedure. In PHP settings, the necessary code for music therapy is G0176. This code is called a "HCPCS" (pronounced "hick-picks") code, from the Healthcare Common Procedure Coding System created by CMS. This national coding system outlines a reporting method for providers when seeking reimbursement for services. Code G0176 is defined as: "Activity therapy, such as music, dance, art or play therapies not for recreation, related to the care and treatment of patient's disabling mental health problems, per session (45 minutes or more)" (Boudrie et al., 2002, p. G Codes-87). Music therapists interested in working in partial hospitalization programs can present this code to employers as a positive way to justify and pay for services in this setting.

Although music therapy has a specific Medicare billing code for PHP only, music therapists need to understand how Medicare payments are made in a variety of settings. Even though therapists do not bill Medicare directly for music therapy in settings other than PHP, music therapy services can contribute to programs that receive Medicare reimbursement. In other words, when a facility asks, "Do you receive Medicare reimbursement?" respond by saying, "Music therapy receives Medicare reimbursement in partial hospitalization programs using a HCPCS code. In other settings, music therapy can contribute to the programs funded through the Medicare PPS system."

What is PPS?

The Prospective Payment System (PPS) was first established by the Social Security Amendments of 1983 as a mechanism for Medicare to reimburse for hospital inpatient services. Under this system, a hospital is paid a fixed amount for each patient regardless of the actual costs incurred. The amount of reimbursement is based upon several factors. The factors that must be addressed include: patient's treatment category, called Diagnosis Related Group (DRG); location of the facility (urban, rural, etc.); percentage of low-income patients the facility serves; whether the facility is a teaching hospital; and whether the particular case is unusually costly. All of these factors are considered core elements of a PPS payment. Each year, basic PPS payment amounts are adjusted (typically upward) by an update factor that is set by Congress. These rate increases are designed to respond to inflation while encouraging facilities to offer cost-effective services (Centers for Medicare and Medicaid, *Providers,* 2003).

In recent years, the PPS method has expanded to other healthcare settings. Following passage of the Balanced Budget Act (BBA) of 1997, a per diem PPS for skilled nursing facilities (SNFs) was started. All costs of services that were covered under Medicare Part A in skilled nursing facilities now fall under a fixed daily reimbursement rate. The BBA of 1997 also authorized the implementation of the PPS for home healthcare services and inpatient rehabilitation facilities (IRFs). In each of these settings, as was noted with inpatient hospital services, specific factors are identified to help determine the final rate of reimbursement.

Under PPS, the DRG or clinical group/category in which a patient's case is placed is the primary factor in establishing the base rate of reimbursement. This classification is based upon information gathered through specific tools. For inpatient rehabilitation facilities, a patient assessment tool (PAI) is utilized to classify patients based on clinical characteristics and expected needs from the program. In skilled nursing facilities, resource utilization groups (RUGs) and the minimum data set (MDS) assessment tool (Centers for Medicare and Medicaid Services, *MDS 2.0 Manuals and Forms,* 2003) are critical components of the Medicare payment system.

Where Does Music Therapy Fit?

Since Medicare payments are pre-set year-to-year based upon factors identified within the related PPS, it is not possible to "bill" for music therapy as a separate service in these healthcare settings. That does not mean, however, that music therapy cannot contribute to the treatment offered and be included within the PPS reimbursement. In fact, music therapists can frequently provide successful interventions that enhance the existing program and ultimately assist the facility in implementing cost-effective services.

Example

An opportunity to develop a music therapy contract with a nursing home occurs and you make an appointment to speak with the facility's Administrator or Director of Nursing. The presentation is well received as these individuals understand the benefits of music therapy programming for residents. They state, "We would love to have you work with our residents but we don't know how to pay for your services. Do you receive Medicare reimbursement?"

Suggested Response

"Currently, the only area where music therapy services are clearly eligible for direct Medicare coverage is in partial hospitalization programs. We are able, however, to contribute to the restorative care program in your facility, documented on the MDS, which can positively affect your reimbursement from Medicare."

Rationale

Restorative care programs are traditionally supervised by nursing personnel and can be implemented by staff members who have the appropriate in-house training and orientation regarding resident care. When attention to restorative services started, implementation often fell to certified nursing assistants (CNAs). Due to busy schedules and staff shortages, some restorative programs were not completed consistently. As a result, many residents were unable to maintain desired levels of independence.

In 2000, AMTA learned that music therapists were more than qualified to provide restorative care programming (Foster, 2000). Several interventions and techniques that music therapists offer in skilled nursing facilities can be considered restorative care. When implementing restorative care programs, there are certain limitations that must be followed. There must be one staff member present for every 4 residents in the group identified as being on a restorative care program. If there are 10 residents participating in music therapy and only 4 are on restorative programs, only one staff member is necessary. If there are 10 residents participating in music therapy and between 5 to 8 individuals are on a restorative program, then there must be two staff members present. The second staff can be a CNA or student/intern, but the additional staff must also be trained in the facility's basic resident care.

MDS Revisions

The MDS 2.0 assessment is currently being revised with plans for a proposed MDS 3.0 to be in use by 2005. AMTA is currently communicating with representatives from CMS and consultants from the RAND Corporation to identify the most effective documentation options for music therapy services within the new MDS 3.0.

Medicare Payment Caps

Another cost-saving mechanism of the Balanced Budget Act of 1997 was a proposal to capitate or "cap" Medicare payments for outpatient physical therapy (PT) and speech therapy (ST) (grouped together) as well as outpatient occupational therapy (OT). Several moratoriums were passed by Congress between 1998 and 2002 to delay implementation of these caps, due to the significant impact the low reimbursement total would have on many Medicare beneficiaries. Despite efforts by the disability community and several large advocacy groups to defer these reimbursement restrictions, the caps went into effect for a brief period beginning September 1, 2003. The caps applied to outpatient services received at therapist and physician offices, outpatient rehabilitation centers, skilled nursing facilities, and home healthcare agencies not covered by Medicare. Outpatient services received in a hospital setting were not included in the cap.

With recent passage of the Medicare reform legislation, however, a new two-year moratorium on these capitated payments was reinstituted, effective December 8, 2003. Although this issue does not affect music therapy directly, future implementation of capitated payments for these therapies has the potential to limit needed services to clients. Advocacy efforts on Capitol Hill will continue in an effort to eliminate these caps completely.

Medicaid

Medicaid, or Title XIX of the Social Security Act, was established in 1965 as an insurance program that is co-financed by the federal and state governments and administered by the states. It is the largest state-based payer of healthcare services for low-income citizens. "Eligibility is limited to low-income people who fall into one of several categories or groups specified in the federal statute" (Perkins & Somers, 2001, p. 1.1). Categories include mandatory categorically needy; optional categorically needy; and medically needy. Some of the groups identified as eligible include individuals over age 65, people with disabilities, pregnant women, and children.

The federal law outlines the basic Medicaid program that all states must provide. Rules regarding eligibility, covered services, participant protections, and implementation are standard throughout all 50 states. Since Medicaid is partially funded by the federal government, these basic federal requirements must be met in order for states to continue receiving these funds. What makes Medicaid so complex, however, is the fact that the federal law also provides options for the states as they implement this program. As each state operates its own programs, it sometimes expands eligibility, increases the number of covered services, and administers the program differently.

There are several minimum benefits that must be provided under the Medicaid system to the categorically needy. Mandatory coverage includes:

- inpatient and outpatient hospital care,
- lab and x-ray services,
- nursing facility care (over age 21),
- Early and Periodic Screening, Diagnosis, and Treatment (EPSDT) services (under age 21),
- pregnancy-related services,
- physician visits, and
- home health services.

The list of optional coverage areas for the categorically needy is much more extensive and is the area in which some music therapists seek reimbursement. This list includes:

- physical therapy and related services,
- intermediate care facility services for individuals with mental retardation or related conditions,
- inpatient psychiatric care,
- hospice,
- case management,
- home and community care for elderly individuals with functionally disabilities,

- community supported living arrangement services,
- alcohol and drug treatment,
- programs of all-inclusive care for the elderly (PACE),
- personal care services,
- respiratory care,
- prosthetic devices, dental services, eyeglasses, and prescription drugs.

Optional coverage under Medicaid also includes another very broad service area that may positively impact access to music therapy interventions. It is defined as:

other diagnostic, screening, preventive, and rehabilitative services, including any medical or remedial services (provided in a facility, home, or other setting) recommended by a physician or other practitioner of the healing arts within the scope of their practice under state law, for the maximum reduction of physical or mental disability and restoration of an individual to the best possible functional level. (Perkins & Somers, 2001, pp. 4.3–4.4)

Although music therapy is not specifically listed under these optional services, the description above provides for consideration of other rehabilitative services as determined by the state. Understanding these federal guidelines will assist music therapists with navigating the Medicaid system within their states.

Coverage areas for the third category of "medically needy" are usually not as generous as noted for the other two categories. The medically needy category allows states to extend Medicaid to individuals who fit within one of the mandatory or optional groups but whose incomes and/or resources are above the eligibility level set by their state. Federal requirements for medically needy include services for children under age 19, prenatal and delivery care for pregnant women, ambulatory care for children, and some home health services. States can extend the medically needy eligibility to other groups and can expand the types of services covered. As of August 2002, 36 states offer some level of Medicaid program for individuals identified as medically needy (Centers for Medicare and Medicaid Services, *Welcome to Medicaid*, 2003).

Medicaid Administration

Knowing the basic coverage areas for Medicaid is just the beginning as you learn about this reimbursement source. Just as every state must meet federal guidelines and define optional eligibility and coverage areas, every state must also follow federal guidelines for program administration and outline state specific methods for implementation.

The Centers for Medicare and Medicaid Services (CMS) are responsible for administration of both the Medicare and Medicaid programs on the federal level. CMS is one agency under the United States Department of Health and Human Service (HHS). As is the case with Medicare, there are several administrative layers involved in the Medicaid program, specifically, federal, regional, state, and local. On the federal level, CMS disseminates regulations and provides guidance to the states through regional CMS offices as well as through direct contact with state Medicaid agencies. Each CMS regional office communicates regularly with the state agencies within its region. Each state designates a single state agency to administer or supervise the Medicaid program. These state agencies then ensure that local agencies and providers adhere to both the state and federal Medicaid regulations.

All states are required to have a written Medicaid plan that must be approved by the Secretary of the Department of Health and Human Services. These state plans must first be reviewed by the governor and then by the CMS regional office before federal funds can be released. It is within this review and approval process that states can request waivers of certain plan requirements in an effort to broaden coverage opportunities. There are three types of Medicaid waivers: freedom of choice waivers, home and community-based care waivers, and demonstration waivers (Perkins & Somers, 2001).

Freedom of Choice Waivers

These waivers, also called Section 1915(b) waivers, are designed to promote cost-effectiveness and efficiency. Approved for two-year periods, these waivers allow states to utilize primary care case management through prepaid managed care programs. The managed care company pays participating providers a monthly fee for each individual enrolled in the program, similar to private insurance managed care agreements. There are quality controls in place so that the program does not conflict with the goals of Medicaid and so states do not restrict access to certain groups.

Home and Community-Based Care Waivers

In recent years, this type of waiver has become the most frequent form of Medicaid reimbursement for music therapy services. Typically, home and community-based care programs are developed to serve individuals who would require institutional placement if services provided through the waiver were not available. In other words, the services funded through the waiver are assisting these individuals to remain in their homes and achieve a level of functioning that helps to prevent institutional placement. With a national emphasis on avoiding institutional placement, many states are pursuing these waivers in an effort to keep citizens in their home communities.

Under this category of waiver, there are three subtypes:

(1) waivers for individuals who would be eligible for Medicaid if institutionalized in a hospital, nursing facility, or intermediate care facility for the mentally retarded and, but for waiver services, would be institutionalized; (2) waivers to provide home and community-based services for the individuals 65 years and older who, but for waiver services, would be likely to require institutional care; and (3) waivers for children under age five who have been infected with AIDS or who are drug dependent at birth. (Perkins & Somers, 2001, p. 2.7)

All three types of home and community-based care waivers may offer coverage of services not available through traditional Medicaid. In addition, covered services can include non-medical support such as personal care, respite care, and homemaking assistance. Service areas can also encompass case management, adult day care, and habilitation. Just as in the freedom of choice waivers, there are quality controls the state must address in order to receive funding for these programs. States must maintain quality through adherence to some or all of the following: provide mechanisms to protect the health and welfare of beneficiaries, be accountable for the money spent; complete evaluations of service need, inform beneficiaries of institutional service alternatives available, document that expenditures are less with the waiver than without, and provide an annual report regarding impact of the waiver.

Demonstration Waivers

Section 1115 of the Social Security Act provides the opportunity for waivers that use demonstration projects to best serve the recipients of Medicaid. During the application process, states address how the projects will "promote the objectives" (Perkins & Somers, 2001, p. 2.7) of the Medicaid program. In order for these waivers to be approved, states must consider how the projects will improve upon the existing service system. In many cases, managed care programs have been introduced as a cost-saving measure of these waivers.

Where Does Music Therapy Fit?

Once you have a basic understanding about how the Medicaid Program works, you can begin to investigate the status of Medicaid reimbursement for music therapy within your state. Although most Medicaid funding for music therapy has come through waiver programs, there are some cases where individual music therapists have successfully applied to be Medicaid providers. Since each state (or territory) has its own regulations, there are obviously over 50 different ways Medicaid is utilized throughout the country. As a result, there is no one way to determine if music therapy can be considered a covered service. But please do not let this information deter you! If all music therapists waited for someone else to "do it first," we would not be able to report any reimbursement success. You won't know until you try!

Example

A case manager from a state regional center contacts you and states she has a 22-year-old female in her caseload diagnosed with autism. She explains that the parents have heard about music therapy and are requesting services to address their daughter's social and leisure skills so that she can remain at home and participate in community activities. The case manager indicates the child receives Medicaid and asks you, "Are you a Medicaid provider?" and/or "Are you covered under the community support waiver?"

Sample Response

"I am not currently a Medicaid provider. This is my first referral for a client receiving Medicaid. I know that some states cover music therapy with Medicaid funding. Let me check into what options are available in our state and I will get back with you next week."

Action Plan

1) Contact the AMTA Reimbursement Committee representative from your region to determine if anyone in your state or region is receiving reimbursement through Medicaid funds.
2) Research the Medicaid program in your state.
   - Determine which state agency administers the Medicaid program.
   - Review the Medicaid regulations on your state's website.
   - Review any and all state regulations that could affect the ability of a music therapist to provide services to and obtain reimbursement from Medicaid beneficiaries, i.e., requirements that all providers be recognized by the state.

- Determine if there are service areas within the state regulations that could include music therapy, i.e., optional coverage for categorically needy, rehabilitation, habilitation, home and community support, PACE, etc.
- Learn if the state utilizes a managed care system for the Medicaid program, and if so, find out the requirements for becoming an approved provider.
- Research the availability of waivers.
- Determine what services are covered by the waivers and who is eligible to utilize waiver funds.

Once you've completed this research, you are ready to pursue direct coverage questions.

- Check the government pages of your phone book for contact numbers. Look under the headings Health and Human Services and/or Social Services.
- If you decide to seek a Medicaid provider number, call your state Medicaid office and request a provider application.
- When they ask what type of provider you are, state your services fall under (the heading within the regulations where music therapy services fit). State you are a qualified music therapist who addresses functional outcomes in that area.
- It's possible that the person answering the phone may state, "We don't pay for music therapy. I can't send you an application."
- If this occurs, ask the individual, "I've received a referral from the regional center in (location). Is there someone in your department I could speak with who could assist me in reviewing other options for funding? Or perhaps you could recommend another department who may also fund services provided through the regional centers?
- If you receive an application, take time to fill it out completely. As with any form of reimbursement, failure to complete the forms accurately can mean the difference between approval and denial.
- Some states' applications are more complex than others. Most states require documentation on treatment goals and areas of functional outcomes you will target through your interventions. This is a good time to review the state regulations and areas of coverage once again to ensure that your services will address the goals the state has established for their Medicaid recipients.
- If you are unable to receive an application, be persistent in talking with other state employees about your situation and explore funding supplied through other health and human services departments within the state. Each state has different names for the various related departments. Keep in mind the needs of the referred client as you seek additional support. Some department examples are Mental Retardation and Developmental Disabilities; Health and Mental Hygiene; Rehabilitation Services; Children, Youth, and Families; etc.
- If your research presents possible reimbursement through a Medicaid waiver, review the coverage areas for inclusion of music therapy.
- Contact the state Medicaid office and request detailed information about the specific waiver.
- If music therapy is listed, request information on how to become an approved provider for the waiver. Most states have an established system for qualifying providers as "vendors"

who accept waiver payment. This usually consists of a brief application and proof of your qualifications/credentials.

- If music therapy is not specifically listed, ask for assistance in determining whether or not music therapy could be covered under the waiver.
- If music therapy is not considered eligible for waiver payment, you do have the option to pursue support from state legislators for inclusion in the waiver program. Be advised that this step will take time and requires detailed planning, involving client families and AMTA Government Relations representatives in your advocacy efforts.

Although Medicaid as a reimbursement source may seem too complicated to tackle, more and more music therapists report some success in accessing state funds to pay for music therapy services. If you are paving the way to Medicaid for the first time in your state, you will probably find some challenges and a few bumps in the road. If you keep the goal of increased access to music therapy as your guide, you will most likely find support along the way that will help you reach your destination of coverage.

Medicaid and IDEA

Another area of Medicaid reimbursement that is complex and sometimes misunderstood is payment for services within special education settings. Children who are eligible for Medicaid and who also receive special education services through the Individuals with Disabilities Education Act (IDEA) are able to access Medicaid funds for some of their IDEA services. The services must be included on the Individual Education Plan (IEP) and must be considered medically necessary to receive Medicaid payment. In addition, it appears that the service must also be recognized by the state as a Medicaid-eligible service, specifically listed within the state Medicaid regulations. In recent years, AMTA has provided information to select states in an effort to increase access to music therapy through this type of funding. At this time (October 2003), however, we are unaware of any states using Medicaid funding to pay for music therapy in special education settings.

Private Insurance

The term *private insurance* encompasses several different products and is supplied by a large number of companies. As evident with Medicare and Medicaid, in order to access funding through these reimbursement sources, you must first understand how they function. This section provides an overview of private insurance types as well as an introduction to the philosophy of managed care.

Thousands of private health insurance plans currently exist across the United States. Many of these companies develop policies and benefit packages similar to those associated with federal programs such as Medicare and Medicaid. Each company must abide by the insurance laws and regulations written by each state. If a company offers coverage in more than one state, it must follow the rules in all the states, even if some requirements are different. To help bring some uniformity to this system, the National Association of Insurance Commissioners, comprised of commissioners from each state, has developed model laws, which it recommends for states to adopt. Although these model laws offer a common thread, each company still establishes its own policies with unique structure and wording (Boni et al., 2000, p. 85).

Nationally recognized insurance companies, such as Blue Cross/Blue Shield, Cigna, and Aetna with different offices in many states, frequently do not provide the same coverage city-to-city, let alone state-to-state. In fact, most health insurance companies offer their subscribers a choice of several different types of plans. These plans can include Traditional Indemnity coverage, Health Maintenance Organization (HMO), Point Of Service (POS), and/or Preferred Provider Organization (PPO), all within one insurance company. There may even be several different benefit packages within each plan and each package may differ even further because of an employer's negotiations with the insurance company. The first plan, traditional indemnity coverage, is a "fee-for-service or 'pay as you go' insurance that has no restrictions on an individual's choice of providers" (Alkire et al., 1995, p. 10). Indemnity coverage is not common in today's healthcare market because this type of plan does not effectively control costs. The latter three plans listed, HMO, POS, and PPO, are examples of managed care, defined as "a controlled method of delivering healthcare services in the most appropriate and cost effective way" (Blount & Waters, 2001, p. 281).

First developed as a way of containing the escalating costs of health care, managed care has become a thriving force in Medicare, Medicaid, and the private insurance industry. The rapid growth of managed care should not be seen as a threat to the music therapy profession; it is simply the structuring of healthcare delivery services integrated with a financing system. It is a systematic approach to providing healthcare services that will offer the most benefit for the cost incurred. As music therapists have often marketed services as being "cost-effective," we are already familiar with the concept behind managed care.

Mechanisms for controlling healthcare costs differ between the various coverage plans, but the process for determining coverage is similar among those plans. For example, most benefit packages require some type of oversight through the use of case managers or gatekeepers. These insurance company representatives are assigned to coordinate services from point of referral to discharge, throughout the continuum of care. In theory, this type of coordination of care will encourage use of preventive medicine and wellness services in an effort to keep healthcare costs down. Once medical treatment is recommended, the case manager examines the services and interventions that could meet the individual's needs and then weighs the overall costs involved in the various interventions to select the best treatment for that client. Other standard aspects of managed care include the need for preauthorization before services are rendered and the need for providers to meet specific credentialing requirements.

Managed care organizations (MCO) are the actual plan types that integrate the financing and delivery of appropriate healthcare services to covered individuals. In all plan types, a select group of providers participates in the program by agreeing to a predetermined and sometimes fixed payment based upon the number of individuals enrolled in a particular program. Traditional indemnity coverage allows individuals to approach their healthcare in a random fashion; an individual can select several providers and those providers may never know they are treating the same client. MCOs offer a systematic approach where the primary care physician, gatekeeper, or case manager coordinates the care in an orderly manner so that all providers involved with one client can communicate with each other about the client's treatment goals and outcomes.

Types of Managed Care Organizations

Health Maintenance Organizations (HMO). An HMO is a health insurance plan that requires members to choose a Primary Care Physician (PCP) from a list of approved providers, to act as a gatekeeper or medical manager for all medical services. Specialist care access is limited and requires a referral from the PCP to specialists listed as approved providers. HMOs pay the primary care physician a fixed rate per month per patient enrolled in that physician's practice, regardless of the amount of services provided. Of all managed care plans, HMOs are the most restrictive. These plans have less expensive premiums but they offer fewer choices in providers and the paperwork involved can be burdensome. It is difficult to seek music therapy reimbursement through HMOs due to the pre-set benefit package and restrictive provider listing.

Preferred Provider Organization (PPO). A PPO is a network of independent physicians, hospitals, and other healthcare providers who contract with an insurance company to provide services at discounted rates. The panel of providers is limited in size but is more extensive than what is offered through HMOs. Most PPOs have some type of utilization review system in place to monitor costs. PPO participants are encouraged to utilize providers within the network in order to receive a higher percentage of coverage. Participants may also select providers that are out-of-network, but incentives are reduced by offering a lower amount of coverage. Because PPOs allow more flexibility and offer a wider selection of providers, the premiums are more expensive than with HMOs. With this flexibility, music therapy coverage is easier to pursue.

Point of Service (POS). A POS offers a combination of HMO and PPO features. Participants do not have to choose how they receive services until they actually need them. Although selection of a Primary Care Physician (PCP) from an approved list is required, participants can elect to utilize providers outside of the network as well. They can decide to stay within the defined HMO part of the plan for 100% coverage or they can choose to see providers outside of the plan for usually 70%–80% coverage. Music therapy reimbursement through POS plans is possible, but the participant may have more out-of-pocket costs due to established co-pays.

Although most potential music therapy clients with insurance are probably enrolled in one form of managed care organization, there are some individuals who have access to the more traditional coverage offered through indemnity plans. These plans provide benefits through a fee-for-service system where payment is made based on the type of service provided. The insurance company does not require use of specific physicians or facilities. One other difference, however, between these types of plans and MCOs is that the participant must usually pay for services and then submit a claim for reimbursement. Since there are no contracts or networks established with the providers, the fees are not negotiated and participants are usually reimbursed at 80% of the total cost after a deductible is met.

Maintaining Quality and Controlling Costs

Although all third party payers address quality and cost within their plans, the private insurance industry has implemented two methods that deserve a closer look. Understanding both case management and provider credentialing will assist music therapists in their efforts to seek reimbursement for the clients they serve.

Case Management. The Case Management Society of America established the following definition of case management: "A collaborative process which assesses, plans, implements, coordinates, monitors, and evaluates optimum services to meet the individual's health needs through communication and available resources to promote quality cost effective outcomes" (Case Management Society of America, 1996). Because of the high cost of providing services to individuals with particular diagnoses, insurance companies frequently assign individuals with certain high dollar diagnoses to case managers. Case managers are typically nurses whose sole purpose is to monitor and coordinate care for the insured individuals. They act as liaisons between the payer and the provider. Case managers are most often advocates for both the insured individuals and the representatives of the healthcare organization in which they work. The case manager is usually the first person a provider comes in contact with at the insurance company. While final decisions are usually made by insurance adjusters, case managers still play a crucial role in the decision making process of the type, scope, frequency, and duration of services that will be provided for specific consumers. Being able to effectively justify the need for a specific service to a case manager is a crucial first step in increasing coverage of music therapy services.

Provider Credentialing. In order for insurance companies to know their enrollees are receiving quality, cost-effective care, they must ensure the providers within their networks are qualified and competent. Depending upon the plan structure and benefit package involved, an insurer determines what type of providers to include in the network, which requires contract agreements. Sometimes these contracts are extended to allied health professionals, especially when companies offer "carve-out" or specialized services in addition to the basic benefit plan. This category of allied health can include music therapy and opens the door for possible contract development between a music therapist and a third-party payer.

Contracts are very important to MCOs for four reasons:

1) They are required by many state and federal regulations.
2) They provide assurances of service availability.
3) They provide a basis for managing costs and utilizing services.
4) They minimize misunderstandings and liability exposure for the MCO. (Stein, 1996, p. 25)

In order for providers to be offered a contract and be included within a network, they must submit an application, which allows a thorough review of their qualifications. Areas that are considered include the following:

1) State Licensure
2) Board Certification
3) Nature and Scope of Clinical Privileges
4) Teaching Affiliations
5) History of Disciplinary Actions
6) Professional Liability Claims
7) Criminal Record (if any)

8) Extent of Malpractice Coverage
9) Practice Profiles: schedule/availability, size of practice, quality assurance efforts
(Stein, 1996, pp. 26–28)

Recognizing not all of these areas apply to music therapists or other allied health professionals, this list can still be beneficial as clinicians prepare for possible questions from the insurance company. Actual contracts between allied health professionals and insurers may outline details such as the following:

1) scope of services to be provided,
2) where services will be provided,
3) responsibilities of the MCO,
4) responsibilities of the providers,
5) procedures to determine enrollee eligibility for services,
6) hours of day during which services will be provided,
7) levels and methods of compensation to the provider,
8) billing procedures to be followed by the provider,
9) provider commitment to protect the confidentiality of enrollee medical information (HIPAA),
10) provider commitment to the MCO's standards of quality service,
11) provider agreement to accept payment from the MCO as payment in full (except for specified copayments),
12) provider agreement to maintain all applicable licenses and certification,
13) provider responsibility to maintain malpractice insurance in accordance with legal and other regulatory requirements (Stein, 1996, pp. 24–32).

Do not let this credentialing and contracting information change your mind about seeking reimbursement for music therapy. These details are presented as an overview of what is required by the industry in general. When services are approved on a case-by-case basis, it is usually not necessary to complete a provider application. Instead of proceeding through the entire credentialing process, many music therapists have successfully received reimbursement by demonstrating education, clinical training, and board certification. Once a relationship develops with one payer, however, it may be worthwhile to pursue "credentialing" and create a contract with them so that access to music therapy services can follow the established referral system.

In general, all managed care programs require providers to be licensed, certified, or registered by the state in which they practice. State recognition of certification for music therapists does not necessarily translate into legislative action. State recognition may only be a matter of public information and education about the music therapy profession's national board certification program. The MT-BC already has been recognized by some third-party payers as meeting requirements for qualified healthcare specialists. Identifying the persons who determine who is eligible for reimbursement and educating them about the profession's national certification program, with particular emphasis on how the CBMT program meets or exceeds the same standards state licensing boards adhere to in test development and administration, may have positive results.

Other Third Party Payers

In addition to traditional reimbursement sources such as Medicare, Medicaid, and private insurance, there are additional sources that offer potential coverage for music therapy services. These programs include: workers' compensation, TRICARE, automobile insurance, adoption subsidy, and state and county programs. Basic knowledge of these other third-party payers may improve access to music therapy for a variety of clients.

Workers' Compensation

To understand workers' compensation benefits, it's important to know that laws exist that provide this type of protection. "Workers' Compensation laws are designed to ensure that employees who are injured or disabled on the job are provided with fixed monetary awards, eliminating the need for litigation" (Petrie et al., 2003, p. 39). Each state has departments or divisions that oversee workers' compensation issues. To assist enforcement, some states also operate several regional offices throughout the state. The actual coverage, however, is provided through private insurance companies that frequently offer traditional healthcare plans as well.

Due to the rising costs of workers' compensation programs, state legislatures have made efforts to require cost containment measures. Insurance companies who offer these programs have implemented these measures through the use of managed care concepts found in the health insurance market. Use of features such as pre-approval and prior authorization before services can be offered, case management, and PPO networks are common among workers' compensation programs.

The benefits of case management in healthcare also apply to case management in workers' compensation. Efforts focus on coordinating the best care while paying close attention to treatment cost-effectiveness. "Because of the emphasis on providing a "holistic" approach to catastrophic cases, case management has been found to be a successful adjunct to workers' compensation programs and appears to have a positive effect on early return to work for beneficiaries" (Alkire et al., 1995, p. 108).

In private insurance situations, music therapists have discovered the benefits of working closely with case managers to determine service coverage. The same holds true for workers' compensation programs. The importance of developing relationships with case managers is significant, regardless of the ultimate reimbursement source. On more than one occasion, case managers employed by insurers processing workers' compensation claims have actually contacted AMTA for lists of qualified music therapists who could provide treatment to the companies' enrollees.

Within the Best Practices section of this manual, reports indicate that this source of reimbursement for music therapy is not just a one-time success. In fact, it appears that coverage under workers' compensation plans may also provide opportunities to expand insurance company recognition of music therapy under general healthcare plans. Since the companies that offer workers' compensation benefits usually offer a full line of insurance products, including traditional and managed care health insurance, evidence of music therapy as a cost-effective service under one plan may positively impact coverage decisions under other company-sponsored plans.

TRICARE

TRICARE is a managed care program of the Department of Defense (DOD) that provides benefits to military personnel, both active and retired, as well as their dependents. Formerly known as the Civilian Health and Medical Program of the Uniformed Services (CHAMPUS), TRICARE was developed to allow service families more choice in how to use their healthcare benefits. Similar to managed care options, TRICARE provides three types of coverage: TRICARE Prime, TRICARE Extra, and TRICARE Standard.

TRICARE Prime is similar to an HMO, where out-of-pocket costs are low but coverage choices are limited. TRICARE Extra is similar to a PPO, where the network of providers is larger than that of the Prime program but more costs are shared with the enrollee. TRICARE Standard is basically designed as the former CHAMPUS program, a fee-for-service program that works like an indemnity plan. Participants in TRICARE Standard usually pay upfront for healthcare services and then submit their own claim forms to receive a percentage of reimbursement (approximately 75%–80%) (Blount & Waters, 2001, pp. 54–57).

Under the same DOD benefit umbrella, CHAMPVA is the Civilian Health and Medical Program of the Veterans Affairs health insurance program. CHAMPVA provides coverage for families of veterans who have service-related disabilities. This program also covers surviving spouses and children of veterans who have died from service-related disabilities. Although all of these DOD programs offer an opportunity for providers to apply for participation in these various benefit plans, non-participating providers can seek reimbursement on a case-by-case basis.

Additional Reimbursement Sources

Within the *Reimbursement Guide for Music Therapists: Phase One,* published by NAMT in 1990, several successful reimbursement case examples were described. Although the healthcare industry has experienced significant change in the 13 years since this guide was first printed, some of the payment sources not associated with traditional health insurance have remained. These other third-party sources that have reimbursed for music therapy services include automobile insurance, adoption subsidy, and state and county boards of mental retardation and/or developmental disabilities.

Access to funds from these additional sources requires music therapists to complete similar steps as the steps required in private insurance reimbursement. Just as the primary structure of music therapy practice (assessment, goal development, interventions, evaluation, and recommendations) follows a systematic method, so does the reimbursement process. Although the terminology and paperwork may be slightly different across these varied sources, similar mechanisms are in place to determine if music therapy can be considered for third-party payment.

Reimbursement Terminology

This section defines basic terminology used in healthcare reimbursement. You may not encounter all of these terms in your efforts to seek coverage for music therapy but all entries are provided as a point of reference.

The definitions were derived from the following sources:

Alkire, A., et al. (1995). *Managed Care: Integrating the Delivery and Financing of Health Care, Part A.* Washington, DC: The Health Insurance Association of America.

Hopkins, J. L., & Casacky, T. (Eds.). (1998). *Managed Care: Integrating the Delivery and Financing of Health Care, Part C.* Washington, DC: The Health Insurance Association of America.

Blount, L. L., & Waters, J. M. (2001). *Mastering the Reimbursement Process* (3rd ed.). United States: American Medical Association.

Stein, J. J. (Ed.). (1997). *Medical Expense Insurance.* Washington, DC: The Health Insurance Association of America.

Active Treatment: A term typically used by insurance companies to ensure that reimbursement for medical/behavioral necessity care will continue as long as therapy is provided with supporting assessment and care planning documentation. Criteria for active treatment includes that 1) the service be furnished under an individualized plan of treatment or diagnosis, 2) there's a reasonable expectation to improve the patient's condition or that the intervention is for diagnostic purposes, and 3) it is supervised and periodically evaluated by a physician.

Actuary: An accredited insurance mathematician who calculates premium rates, dividends, and reserves, and prepares statistical studies and reports.

Allowable Charge: The maximum fee that a third-party payer will use to reimburse a provider for a given service.

Ancillary Services: Healthcare services conducted by providers other than primary care physicians.

Assignment of Benefits: Provision in a health benefits claim form by which the client directs the insurer to pay the provider directly for any benefits that are available.

Authorizations: Consent or endorsement by a primary care physician for patient referral to ancillary services and specialists.

Balance Billing: A billing practice where providers bill patients for charges that remain after the insurer has reimbursed the provider a set payment rate. Many managed care plans do not allow the use of balance billing and may penalize providers who use this method in their practices.

Billable Charge: A healthcare product or service that is covered under an insurance contract.

Billing Forms: Forms completed by practitioners to bill for services.

    CMS 1500—A universal claim form, developed by Centers for Medicare and Medicaid Services (CMS), for healthcare providers to use in billing insurance carriers.

Capitation: A managed care method of payment where a physician or hospital is paid a fixed amount for each enrolled healthcare plan member regardless of the actual number or type of services provided to these individuals.

Carve-Out: Term used to describe certain services that are not included in standard benefits and that are paid for separately on a pre-determined fee-for-service basis. Programs that may be offered as carve-outs include behavioral health, prescription drugs, and dental coverage.

Case Management: An arrangement in which a "case manager" who is typically not a physician (usually an RN or MSW) serves as a medical manager responsible for coordinating the care process for selected consumers. Case managers frequently work with patients who have expensive conditions, but they are also involved in approving numbers of visits for on-going treatment for other patients as well. Case managers have two goals: containing costs and promoting the use of more effective interventions to meet patient needs.

Cost Benefit Analysis: A method of measuring the benefits expected from a proposed treatment, calculating the costs of that treatment, and then determining whether the benefits outweigh the costs. In healthcare, cost-benefit analysis involves comparing the costs of medical care with the economic benefits of the care. Third-party payers look at the actual dollar amount of the care and the dollar amount of the benefits. Benefits usually include reduced future healthcare costs and increased earnings due to improved health of those receiving the care.

Credentialing: The practice by insurers of reviewing the qualifications of providers before allowing them to be included in insurance plan networks. The process requires an extensive examination of a provider's licensure, malpractice history, analysis of practice patterns, and certification.

Diagnostic Codes: Codes required by insurance companies when seeking reimbursement.

    ICD-9-CM: International Classification of Diseases, 9th revision, clinical modification. This book includes classification of disease by diagnosis and listed as alphanumeric codes. You might have seen these codes on the back of a billing form from your own physician; every time you visit the doctor, one of these codes is used to code the current diagnosis.

    ICD-10-CM (10th revision) in draft form is available but not yet adopted for use.

Evidence-Based Medicine: The systematic selection of clinical processes and interventions, based on research studies that offer the greatest degree of confidence in their conclusions. The information is then compiled into treatment protocols designed to decrease medical costs and maintain or improve healthcare quality.

Fee-For-Service: Method of payment for healthcare services that is based on each visit or service provided.

Fee Schedule: The maximum dollar amount allowed for services that are provided under a specific contract.

Fiscal Intermediary (FI): A person or organization that serves as another's financial agent. They process claims, provide services, and issue payments on behalf of certain private, federal, and state health benefit programs or other insurance organizations. For instance, providers of healthcare select public or private FIs, which enter into an agreement with the secretary of the Department of Health and Human Services (HHS) under Part A of Medicare to pay claims and perform other functions. For instance, Blue Cross/Blue Shield of various states frequently is the FI for Medicare claims. A complete list of all FIs and Medicare carriers can be found at: www.cms.hhs.gov/contacts/incardir.asp

Gatekeeper: Title frequently given to primary care physicians as they strive to control healthcare service utilization and specialist referrals for HMO participants.

Health Insurance Portability and Accountability Act (HIPAA): 1996 federal law that requires plans to guarantee coverage to any member of an enrolled group, regardless of his or her current or past health status; requires some plans to provide parity between mental health and other health benefits; guarantees the right of at least a 48-hour stay for maternity admissions; mandates medical record privacy regulations including rules for electronic billing.

Health Plan Employer Data and Information Set (HEDIS): A national standardized method for measuring aspects of managed care organizations, such as quality of care, member access, satisfaction, and financial stability.

National Committee for Quality Assurance (NCQA): Private, voluntary accrediting organization for managed care. It assures quality, credentialing, utilization management, customer rights, preventive health services, and medical records. Developed and oversees the Health Plan Employer Data and Information Set (HEDIS).

Negotiated Fees: Managed care plans and providers mutually agree on a set fee for each service. This negotiated rate is usually based on services defined by the Current Procedural Terminology (CPT®) Codes, generally at a discount from what the provider would usually charge. Providers cannot charge more than this fee.

Network Providers: Limited group or panel of providers that participates in a managed care plan. Insurance plan enrollees may be required to use network providers exclusively or they may be allowed to use providers outside of the network for a higher fee.

Outcomes Measurement: The process of systematically tracking a client's clinical treatment and responses to that treatment, including measures of functional status, for the purpose of improving care.

Per Diem Rate: A fixed all inclusive price for one day of hospital or skilled nursing facility care, which includes all supplies and services provided during that day, except for physicians' fees. This payment method is different than a "per episode" rate of payment where one lump sum of money is paid per episode of care, for example, when one flat fee is paid for an entire hospital admission.

Pre-authorization (also known as preadmission certification, prior approval, pre-certification, prior authorization or PA): The process of obtaining certification or authorization from the health plan for care/services and routine hospital admissions. Failure to obtain pre-authorization often results in a denial of the claim.

Primary Care Physician (PCP): Primary manager of an individual's health care. The PCP concept is central to controlling costs and utilization within managed care. The PCP provides basic care to the enrollee, initiates referrals to specialists, and provides follow-up care. Refers exclusively to other contracted providers and admits patients only to contracted hospitals. Usually defined as a physician practicing in such areas as internal medicine, family practice, and pediatrics.

Procedural Codes: Codes required by insurance companies for reimbursement that describe the service provided.

   CPT®: Current Procedural Terminology—This coding manual is published by the American Medical Association with classification by care procedure. Each year these codes are reviewed, updated and revised. Please refer to page 21 for detailed information on CPT® Codes.

   HCPCS: Healthcare Common Procedure Coding System—Includes level 1 (CPT®) and level 2 (alphanumeric codes for reporting most medical services and supplies provided to Medicare and Medicaid patients). The activity therapy code for Medicare coverage in partial hospitalization programs is included in this manual. (G0176).

PPS: Prospective Payment System—The method of third-party payment by which rates of payment to healthcare providers for services to patients are established in advance for the coming fiscal year. Providers are paid these rates for services delivered regardless of the cost actually incurred in providing these services. PPS has been around for awhile, basically since 1983 when DRGs or Diagnostic Related Groups were implemented (for example, if a patient was admitted with a cardiac arrest, he/she was allowed a set amount of hospital days; if the patient stayed after those days elapsed, the hospital had to cover the additional costs.) PPS has been implemented in skilled nursing facilities, hospice, and in-patient rehab settings.

TRICARE: Nationwide Department of Defense (DOD) managed care program, operated in partnership with civilian contractors, that is designed to ensure high-quality consistent healthcare benefits, preserve beneficiaries' choice of healthcare providers, improve access to care, and contain healthcare costs. The program offers a choice of a HMO, PPO, or a fee-for-service program (the former CHAMPUS program).

UCR: Usual, Customary, and Reasonable—The average charge for a similar service offered by providers in a specific geographical area.

Waivers: Term usually associated with the Medicare or Medicaid programs where the government waives certain regulations or rules for a managed care or insurance program. These waivers are usually limited to a specific patient population and/or a specific geographic area. There are currently a few states that allow payment for music therapy services through use of Medicaid waivers with certain client groups. A few other states are reviewing the possibility of including music therapy in these programs.

CPT® Codes

CPT® (Current Procedural Terminology) is a systematic listing and coding of procedures and services performed by physicians, therapists, or other healthcare professionals in clinical practice. This coding system was developed by the American Medical Association (AMA) and is utilized by the majority of insurance companies for reimbursement purposes. All music therapists should become familiar with CPT® codes. Coding information can be found in the *CPT® Standard/ Professional Edition* manual, available for purchase through the American Medical Association by calling 1-800-621-8335. The 2004 edition prices range from $57.95–$82.95. The manual is updated each year, making it very important to check for any changes in codes used on a regular basis (*Current Procedural Terminology (CPT®) 2004 Professional Edition*, 2003).

Basically, a code is assigned for therapeutic procedures that accurately and specifically identify the exact service being performed. Each code is identified with a 5-digit number.

How do CPT® codes pertain to music therapy? Most case managers and insurance companies consider the CPT® codes manual the reference of choice. The insurance company will reimburse for the therapy or service rendered based on a dollar amount per code. In addition, this code number may designate a 15-minute block of time. If a therapist is performing a specific service for one hour, then that code number would be used and the dollar amount multiplied times four. In one therapy hour, a therapist may use two or three different codes, and each code may be assigned a different dollar amount.

Currently, there are insurance companies that are reimbursing for prescribed music therapy services once certain CPT® codes have been approved by a case manager, utilization review director, or an insurance adjuster. ***Please remember:*** Currently, in order to bill insurance companies for music therapy, CPT® codes must be ***APPROVED*** prior to rendering the service. Typically, due to managed care, many clients in the United States today are subject to case management. Insurance companies' case managers have the control to approve or disapprove a certain service or CPT® code. It is essential for music therapists to effectively communicate with clients' case managers when seeking reimbursement.

On pages 24–25, you will find the CPT® codes that music therapists have used to seek reimbursement for their services. The listed codes have been found to be the most effective codes currently available to describe a variety of music therapy treatment interventions. These codes are not discipline specific and are also used by related healthcare professionals (i.e., physical, occupational, speech, and recreational therapy). It is advised that clinicians do not submit bills using the same codes as another discipline for treatment on the same day, as that would appear to be duplication of services. Even though the interventions are different, the procedure codes are broadly defined and could be interpreted by someone processing the claim to be repetition of service. It is extremely important to communicate with other therapists involved in the client's treatment so you can adhere to proper billing procedures.

The Process of Reimbursement

When seeking reimbursement from private insurance companies, there are specific recommended steps that, if followed carefully, should increase your opportunities for success. Although each company has a different method for benefit determination, the overall process of seeking coverage for music therapy is very similar company to company. Due to the diversity in insurance plans, it is necessary for music therapists to examine reimbursable situations on a case-by-case basis. Preauthorization is standard among most third-party payers, as it pertains to authorizing certain forms of medical treatment. Therapists must receive prior approval for each intervention they plan on billing to the insurance company. Clinicians should view the preauthorization process as an opportunity to educate payers about the benefits of music therapy and the qualification standards of music therapists. Attention to the steps outlined in this section will provide guidance through this process of pursuing insurance reimbursement for music therapy interventions.

Step One: Referrals

Referrals can come from a variety of sources such as physicians, psychologists, social workers, case managers, and other related healthcare professionals, as well as parents, friends and clients themselves. Frequently referrals are received verbally, in an informal manner, through a phone call or team meeting. At other times, the referral can be received in a formal manner, written, for example, on a prescription pad from a physician. Once the referral is received, what do you do?

Step Two: Collect Insurance Information

Regardless of who sent the referral, the next step in the reimbursement process is to collect insurance information from the prospective client so you can determine benefits. In some cases, the therapist may already know the client and may be pursuing reimbursement at the client's and/or family's request. In other cases, the referral is to a new client and the therapist will need to determine necessity of treatment and collect insurance information through an initial meeting and evaluation. This step can seem awkward because you need information about the client's treatment goals before calling the insurance company—but at the same time you need to call the insurance company to seek coverage before you can assess the client's treatment goals! Which comes first?

Obviously, a therapist must meet with the potential client to assess needs, goals, and functional outcomes before pursuing reimbursement. Some therapists charge either a minimal amount or pro-rate fees for the initial meeting/evaluation, choosing to include compensation for that evaluation as part of a full assessment later billed to the insurance company. Other therapists charge a full session or assessment fee, with clients initially paying out-of-pocket. Clients are then responsible for seeking reimbursement for the initial assessment once approval for treatment is received. Each therapist must consider the administrative tasks involved in seeking reimbursement when setting fees for his/her practice. Whatever method is developed to address this initial assessment and before treatment proceeds, therapists need to collect the specific information identified on the Music Therapy Treatment Prior Approval Form (page 46). If possible, make a copy of the client's insurance card for future reference. Information requested on this prior approval form will assist you as you initiate communication with the insurance company. Prior to contacting the insurance company, complete the first section on the form and obtain the phone number for benefit verification.

During the initial evaluation, it is important to discuss with the client and/or the family your fee structure and billing methods, especially in the event the insurance company refuses coverage or denies payment. To ensure you will be paid for services rendered, you should obtain signatures on an assignment of benefits/release of medical information form. This form (sample on page 47) allows the insurance company to pay you, the provider, directly. It also states that the client (or guardian) is financially responsible for all charges whether or not payment is received from the insurance company. This form can also serve as an authorization for release of medical information necessary to process the insurance claim.

What About HIPAA?

The Health Insurance Portability and Accountability Act of 1996 is a law that "mandates policies and protections for confidentiality of electronically transmitted medical information" (Blount & Waters, 2001, p. 279). "Covered entities" as defined by the law "refers to 1) A health plan. 2) A healthcare clearinghouse. 3) A healthcare provider who transmits any health information in electronic form in connection with a transaction . . ." (Hubbard, Glover, & Hartley, 2003, p. 472). Most music therapists are not considered "covered entities" by the U.S. Department of Health and Human Services' (HHS) Office for Civil Rights, and, as such, do not need to meet the HIPAA privacy rules, which went into effect April 2003. In addition, few, if any, music therapists submit bills to the Centers for Medicare and Medicaid services electronically, which exempts them from being covered entities under the transaction rules effective October 2003.

Problems may occur, however, when therapists attempt to contact a client's insurance company to verify benefits and pursue reimbursement. Even though you may have received a signature on the release of information form, the insurance company may require that the insured provide verification of giving you permission to discuss coverage. One solution may be to call the insurance company while you are with the client or family so that verbal consent can be given over the phone. Even though you are not a "covered entity" under HIPAA regulations, the insurer

CPT® CODES

CODE #	TITLE	DESCRIPTION
97110	Therapeutic Procedure, one or more areas, each 15 minutes	Therapeutic exercises to develop strength and endurance, range of motion and flexibility
97112	Neuromuscular Re-education	Of movement, balance, coordination, kinesthetic sense, posture, and/or proprioception for sitting and/or standing activities
97113	Aquatic Therapy with Therapeutic Exercises	
97116	Gait Training	Includes stair climbing
97150	Therapeutic Procedure(s), Group (2 or more individuals)	Group therapy procedures involve constant attendance of the physician or therapist, but by definition do not require one-on-one patient contact by the physician or therapist
97530	Therapeutic Activities (one-on-one), each 15 minutes	Direct patient contact by the provider (use of dynamic activities to improve functional performance)
97535	Self Care/Home Management Training, each 15 minutes	Activities of daily living (ADL) and compensatory training, meal preparation, safety procedures, and instructions in use of assistive technology devices/adaptive equipment; direct one-on-one contact by provider
97537	Community/Work Reintegration Training, each 15 minutes	Shopping, transportation, money management, avocational activities and/or work environment/ modification analysis, work task analysis; use of assistive technology device/adaptive equipment, direct one-on-one contact by provider
97542	Wheelchair Management/ Propulsion Training, each 15 minutes	
97139	Unlisted Therapeutic Procedure	Specify

CODE #	TITLE	DESCRIPTION
97532	Development of Cognitive Skills (one-on-one), each 15 minutes	Improve attention, memory, problem solving (includes compensatory training), direct patient contact by the provider
97533	Sensory Integrative Techniques (one-on-one), each 15 minutes	Enhance sensory processing and promote adaptive responses to environmental demands, direct patient contact by the provider
97799	Unlisted Physical Medicine–Rehabilitation Service or Procedure	
96105	Assessment of Aphasia (per hour)	Includes assessment of expressive and receptive speech and language function, language comprehension, speed production ability, reading, spelling, writing (e.g., by Boston Diagnostic Aphasia Examination) with interpretation and report
96110	Developmental Testing	Limited (e.g., Developmental Screening Test II, Early Language Milestone Screen), with interpretation and report
96111	Extended Assessment (per hour)	Includes assessment of motor, language, social, adaptive and/or cognitive functioning by standardized developmental instruments (e.g., Bayley Scales of Infant Development) with interpretation and report
96115	Neurobehavioral Status Exam (per hour)	Clinical assessment of thinking, reasoning and judgment (e.g., acquired knowledge, attention, memory, visual spatial abilities, language functions, planning), with interpretation and report
92506	Evaluation of Speech	Evaluation of speech, language, voice, communication, auditory processing, and/or aural rehabilitation status
92507	Treatment of Speech; individual	Treatment of speech, language, voice, communication, and/or auditory processing disorder (includes aural rehabilitation)

may require a signed copy of the release form as well as a signed copy of any standard company privacy/authorization forms in order to meet their HIPAA requirements.

Point of information: If in your private practice you develop contracts with larger healthcare agencies that are bound by HIPAA rules, it may be in your best interest to create your own privacy notices to ease the process of receiving referrals and working with these agencies. Clinicians in these situations may be considered "business associates" under the HIPAA rules. It is our understanding that "business associates" do need to abide by the privacy rules and establish privacy notices for their clients. To address this need, a sample HIPAA privacy statement and sample release forms will be available on the members-only section of the AMTA website for clinicians to use as a guide.

Step Three: Determine Client Needs

Once you've completed an initial assessment and collected the basic insurance information, you must determine treatment recommendations. You need to define the scope, duration, and frequency of proposed music therapy treatment before communicating with the potential payer. Based upon findings from the assessment, develop specific treatment goals and identify music therapy strategies that will be implemented. Next, determine how many sessions will be needed to achieve these goals. When presenting the request for number of sessions and the timeline for the sessions, be aware that the insurer will want to periodically re-evaluate the client's progress to determine if treatment is still necessary. It is important to establish realistic goals and a realistic time frame when negotiating for reimbursement.

Keep in mind that initial approval for payment may be for a brief period, perhaps one to two sessions per week, for 6 to 8 weeks. At the conclusion of those 6 to 8 weeks, the payer will want to review the progress before approving additional treatment. Therapists reporting successful outcomes often receive continued approval for longer periods, anywhere from 12 weeks to several months. Obviously, devoting sufficient time at the beginning of this process to create the goals, methods, and treatment timeline will prove very beneficial in the long run.

Medical/Behavioral Necessity

While developing treatment recommendations, one issue that must be considered is why you or the referring individual believes music therapy treatment is "medically or behaviorally necessary." Medical/behavioral necessity is the reasonable and necessary medical treatment and services needed for an individual diagnosed with a specific medical condition. In other words, it's a treatment or intervention that is appropriate for the client's diagnosis, and, if not provided, it would adversely affect the client's condition or the quality of care the client receives.

This definition can vary tremendously depending upon the insurer. A doctor's order alone does not make it medically or behaviorally necessary. This fact that there is so much variance among insurance plans about what is medically or behaviorally necessary has led to much public debate and multiple legal battles. In a recent publication from the United States Department of Health and Human Services (HHS)–Substance Abuse and Mental Health Services Administration (SAMHSA), the authors reviewed industry information on this issue. Five dimensions were identified within insurers' definitions of medical and behavioral necessity that determine possible benefit areas. These dimensions include:

1) Contractual scope—Does the insurance plan allow payment for the services recommended? Does the plan allow coverage for only treatment of illness or does it also cover treatments that assist with maintaining and improving functional abilities?

2) Is the treatment in accord with professional standards of practice?

3) Does the treatment provide for client safety and is it provided in an appropriate setting?

4) Is the treatment medical in nature and not just for the client's convenience?

5) What is the cost? Is the treatment cost-effective? Will the benefits outweigh the costs? Will goals be achieved in a shorter amount of time than another recommended treatment?

(Rosenblaum, Kamoie, Mauery, & Walitt, 2003)

Although the insurance company case manager or claims reviewer will make the final determination about whether or not a service is medically/behaviorally necessary based on company policy, your assessment should justify the need for music therapy in these terms. Documentation of treatment needs, along with specific plans and measurable goals, is crucial. Sometimes this information is sufficient and the company won't require additional treatment justification.

If asked to present more information, however, in order to establish medical/behavioral necessity, be prepared to submit the following documentation:

- Client's diagnosis and current medical condition that the therapist will address.
- Medical information to substantiate the need for recommended treatment/service.
- Location and estimated beginning and ending dates of recommended treatment/service.
- Name and credentials of provider performing the treatment.
- Outline of treatment plan and outcome-based, measurable goals.
- Concise and clear statements of why the recommended treatment/service will be beneficial for this client.

Once interventions begin, be sure to watch for patient plateaus where custodial or maintenance issues might be questioned. When documentation demonstrates a client is not continuing to make progress, insurers take notice and consider this lack of progress a "red flag," indicating that perhaps the service should no longer receive reimbursement.

Step Four: Prepare Marketing Materials

A critical step in the reimbursement process involves preparation of educational and public relations material related to music therapy. Most clinicians have developed this type of material for potential employers, clients, and the general public. Public relations materials available from AMTA can provide guidance as you develop your own marketing package. The AMTA fact sheet (pages 60–61), originally developed for education and advocacy with U.S. Senators and Representatives during Hill Day events, is also a good resource to utilize.

For reimbursement purposes, printed information should be concise with attention to research and case examples of music therapy with the client's diagnosis or disability. If specific research is limited, gather supportive documentation in related treatment areas. For example, instead of presenting research focused on a particular diagnosis, present research focused on identified problem areas such as attention and motivation, speech and motor skills, social skills, cognitive skills, etc.

Marketing materials should also include the following:

1) *Music therapy definition:* Create a personal definition that describes your practice and experience.

Sample language to use as a guide:

> Music therapy is a well-established, research-based health profession in which music is used within a therapeutic relationship to address physical, emotional, cognitive, and social needs of individuals of all ages. Music therapists use both instrumental and vocal music strategies to facilitate changes that are non-musical in nature. After assessment of the strengths and needs of each client, qualified music therapists provide indicated treatment and participate as members of the interdisciplinary team to support a vast continuum of outcomes. Employment may be in general hospitals, nursing homes, rehabilitation facilities, mental health agencies, hospice programs, forensic settings, out-patient clinics, public and private schools, and may take the form of a contractual/consulting private practice.

2) *Brief overview of how the healthcare industry recognizes music therapy:* Recognition of a profession within the healthcare industry is very important to payers. This is why all music therapists must understand which agencies, regulations, and accreditation standards acknowledge music therapy as a health profession.

Sample language to use as a guide:

> The Centers for Medicare and Medicaid Services (CMS) recognize music therapy as a reimbursable service in partial hospitalization settings using HCPCS Code G0176. (Boudrie et al., 2002)

> Music therapy is listed as a rehabilitation therapy, code 93.84, in the *International Classification of Diseases, 9th Revision, Clinical Modification (ICD-9-CM) Manual (Sixth Edition).* (Hart & Hopkins, 2003)

> The Joint Commission on Accreditation of Healthcare Organizations (JCAHO) recognizes music therapists as qualified individuals who may provide services within accredited facilities. Music therapy's professional association, the American Music Therapy Association (AMTA), is a member of JCAHO's Professional Organization Liaison Network. AMTA also represents the National Coalition of Creative Arts Therapies Associations (NCCATA) to JCAHO's, Professional and Technical Advisory Committees (PTACs) which review and discuss JCAHO standards. NCCATA's involvement with the PTACs is through its membership in the Coalition of Rehabilitation Therapy Organizations (CRTO). Other CRTO members include the American Physical Therapy Association, American Occupational Therapy Association, American Speech-Language-Hearing Association, American Therapeutic Recreation Association and The National Therapeutic Recreation Society.

AMTA is also an Associate member of CARF's (the Rehabilitation Accreditation Commission) Board of Trustees. Whether as part of creative arts therapies or alone, music therapy is recognized by both JCAHO and CARF within certain standards manuals.

3) *Qualifications required to practice music therapy:* It is very important to include information about board certification in your marketing package. The Certification Board for Music Therapists has supportive material you can present that explains the professional credential required by the profession. Please utilize CBMT's public relations materials to emphasize the value of this national practice exam. Further information regarding board certification may be obtained by contacting the CBMT at 1-800-765-CBMT, or through the website: www.cbmt.org

Sample language to use as a guide:

The MT-BC (Music Therapist-Board Certified) is issued by the Certification Board for Music Therapists (CBMT), an independent, non-profit corporation fully accredited by the National Commission for Certifying Agencies. The CBMT programs meet or exceed the same standards licensing boards adhere to in test development and administration. The MT-BC is granted by the CBMT to an individual upon a) successful completion of an AMTA approved academic and clinical training program, and b) successful completion of a written objective national examination demonstrating current skills in the profession of music therapy; and is maintained through recertification every five years through reexamination or upon the successful completion and documentation of 100 Continuing Music Therapy Education credits.

Point of information: While some disciplines require that providers be licensed by the state in order to receive third-party reimbursement, this has not been the case for music therapy. Board certified music therapists, without state licenses in related fields, have successfully obtained third-party reimbursement for their services.

In addition to the marketing tools described above, it is recommended you develop a personal portfolio, which includes a copy of your resume and/or curriculum vita. Some of the insurance company representatives you talk with may not know anything about music therapy. Your resume and CV present the education, clinical training, and continuing education involved in the profession. Although it may not always be necessary to provide this documentation to the payer, it's wise to be prepared with an updated version.

Step Five: Seek Written Referral from Primary Care Physician

With documented permission from the client and/or family, contact the primary care physician (PCP) to obtain a referral for music therapy. In many cases, the initial referral may not have come directly from the PCP. This step is crucial to the pre-approval process. Be prepared to present your treatment goals and marketing materials to educate the physician on the outcomes that will be addressed through music therapy. Although a direct referral from the PCP may not be required according the particular insurance plan, having the referral from the PCP will be helpful in seeking reimbursement. Talking with the physician can also be helpful in determining the appropriate diagnostic code (ICD-9-CM) to use in the billing process. It is best to utilize the code recommended by the PCP.

Step Six: Call the Insurance Company

Now that all your documentation is complete, it is time to call the insurance company. During the first call to verify benefits, please remember that the person answering the phone is probably a customer service agent who does not have any specialized training in health care. It's not unusual for this individual to be unaware of music therapy as a treatment option. Using the Music Therapy Treatment Prior Approval Form as a guide, fill out as much of the form as possible. It may be that the person answering the phone will be unable to provide all the information you are seeking. If this occurs, politely ask to speak to a case manager or someone who can provide assistance with your request. Don't be discouraged if it takes a few calls to get the information needed to proceed. Throughout all calls to the insurance company, remember to remain professional.

Step Seven: Obtain Prior Approval

The next step in the process follows closely behind or at the same time as the first call to the payer. If you are able to talk with a case manager or other decision maker within the company, you may be able to obtain pre-approval during the first call. If a case manager has not been assigned to your client, you may request the company provide one so that a determination of coverage can be made based upon the client's needs and the treatment outcomes you will address.

In talking with the case manager or company representative, present the referral, assessment findings, treatment goals, supportive research, music therapy overview, and your qualifications. Be prepared to provide justification of the treatment's medical or behavioral necessity. Discuss the functional outcomes you will address and request pre-approval for treatment using appropriate CPT® codes that best describe the recommended music therapy procedures. Include in your request the number of sessions and corresponding timeline recommended. Offer to fax, e-mail, or mail supportive material to assist in the pre-approval process.

Obtain verbal approval if possible, and if not, follow through with any requests for additional information. If approval is received, ask for the payment rate associated with the CPT® codes presented and determine if the rate is reasonable. If the reimbursement amount does not appear close to your standard rates, determine if the payment rates are negotiable. Request how often the company wants to be billed (i.e., after every session, after a certain number of sessions, or after all approved sessions are complete.) Also during this discussion, be sure to ask how often to send clinical updates and document the name, title, department, address, phone and fax numbers, and e-mail where these updates must be sent. Maintain this reporting schedule!

Point of information: When determining standard rates, it is recommended that music therapists consult with small business advisors and/or accountants to assist in establishing appropriate professional fees. The full range of cost factors should be considered so that "usual, customary, and reasonable" rates reflect the quality of the music therapy services provided.

Step Eight: Send Confirmation Letter

If you receive verbal approval, always follow up with written confirmation. Using the Approval Confirmation Letter Template as a guide (page 48), prepare a letter to be sent to the case manager or medical review staff to confirm the approval received over the phone. The template defines all the data that should be included when confirming pre-approval.

If unable to obtain pre-approval by phone as discussed in Step Seven, you may need to contact the insurance company though the mail by using the Prior Approval Letter Template (page 49), as a guide. This template presents assessment information for the first time. In other words, everything that would have been covered during a phone call with a case manager is introduced through this letter format. In some situations, it may be necessary to approach the payer in this manner. If you must submit the pre-approval request through written documentation, make sure to include all the elements listed on the template. It is also important to remember to follow up within two weeks after sending this letter, as your request may not receive immediate attention.

Step Nine: Provide Music Therapy Treatment

Upon successful completion of Steps One through Eight, music therapy interventions can finally begin! Actually, those first eight steps can be completed over a brief period of time so that reaching Step Nine does not have to seem like a long-range goal. Throughout treatment, be sure to document all elements of the program, such as assessment, intervention descriptions, cost-effectiveness, treatment effectiveness, and achievement of goals and functional outcomes.

As with all music therapy services, therapists should take extreme care in how they document. If services are being provided outside of a facility through a private practice, the music therapist should create a chart for each client. Whether sessions are presented privately or as part of a facility program, chart entries are expected for each encounter with the client. Each chart entry should include observation of the individual's current status, observations of the individual's responses to the current interventions, and observations of the individual's response to treatment as it relates to the individualized treatment goals. Entries should be typed, or legible if hand-written, and worded in a way that allows data to be understood by non-music therapists.

To emphasize the importance of meticulous documentation in healthcare, it may be helpful to review the overall purpose of this documentation.

- Provide a legal record of the client's condition and the course of therapeutic intervention from admission to discharge.
- Serve as an information source for patient (client) care.
- Facilitate communication among healthcare professionals who contribute to the patient's care.
- Furnish data for use in treatment, education, research, and reimbursement (Care Communications, Inc., n.d.).

Since documentation is a legal record of the therapeutic intervention, it is essential that it be all of the following: organized, legible, concise, clear, accurate, complete, current, objective (rather than opinionated), and that it have correct grammar and spelling. (Care Communications, Inc., n.d.).

Remaining thorough as you implement the approved interventions will be invaluable to receiving third-party payment. It may seem like a lot of paperwork at first, but in the long run, it will make the business end of your practice much more manageable.

Key Points:
- Document all interventions.
- Evaluate individual client progress.
- Collect data on treatment outcomes.
- Maintain contact with case manager.
- Present clear and accurate information.
- Respond to all communication in a timely and professional manner.

Step Ten: Complete Billing/Claim Submission Worksheet

As you approach completion of the approved number of sessions or the end of the negotiated timeline, fill out the information on the Billing/Claim Submission Worksheet found on pages 50–51. This worksheet will help you prepare for submitting the actual claim for payment. Be advised that some content areas are similar to content areas on the Music Therapy Prior Approval Form. This worksheet, however, also provides space to list specific diagnosis and billing code details, which are required for successful reimbursement. As with the other sample forms included in this manual, it is provided as a guide for you to customize to your situation.

As successful reimbursement for music therapy is frequently approved on a case-by case basis, each case may require a different schedule for submitting claims. Be sure to submit claims in the time frame outlined by the payer during the pre-approval process.

Step Eleven: Submit Claim

All the attention to details and the efforts to be thorough during this entire reimbursement process will be extremely helpful as you submit the actual claim for payment. Believe it or not, sometimes payment is delayed or denied just because a claim was filed incorrectly or was not complete. Don't lose focus now!

Although you may have prepared a specialized invoice developed for your individual practice, most insurers also require you to submit a CMS 1500 form. As defined on page 18, the CMS 1500 form is the standardized form used in Medicare billing but also accepted by many private insurance companies for individual claims. A copy of the CMS 1500 can be found on pages 52–53. The original of this form uses a scannable red ink, as some insurance companies scan the claims to process them more rapidly. It is advised that you obtain original copies for use in your practice, even though in the case of music therapy, these claims will probably be processed manually. Copies of the CMS 1500 form can be purchased from the U.S. Government Printing Office, 202-512-1800.

The following website address—http://www.cms.hhs.gov/providers/edi/edi5.asp—is a good resource for detailed information on completing the CMS 1500 form. Although the site focuses on Medicare billing, the site also provides links to guidance language for completing this standardized form. Code number entries are required for some sections, such as place of service and type of service. The website listed above provides the necessary code definitions for review and selection. As previously mentioned, attention to simple things on this form like correct spelling and having the complete address of client may make the difference between being paid in a timely manner and having your claim denied.

Claim Payment Checklist:
- Submit valid codes
  - Diagnosis – (ICD-9-CM)
    - List the primary diagnosis first
    - List the specific condition you are treating as the secondary code
  - Procedure – (CPT®)
    - Use the procedure code that accurately describes the treatment
- Submit standard claim forms (CMS-1500)
- Include copies of documentation
  - Clinical information
    - Assessment
    - Treatment goals
    - Description of interventions
    - Progress notes
    - Evaluation of outcomes
  - Prior approval information
    - Confirmation letter
  - Referral from primary care physician

Step Twelve: Follow-up with Payer

Reaching Step Twelve can be cause for celebration as well as an opportunity to continue communication with the insurance company. In this final stage, the positive result of all your hard work is that reimbursement for music therapy services is sent in a timely manner. Take a moment to correspond with the case manager or representative that approved treatment to extend thanks for his/her assistance on your client's behalf, noting progress and outcomes achieved. This is also an opportunity to offer your expertise for any future clients in their care who could benefit from music therapy.

Even if all steps are followed diligently, don't be discouraged if your claim is denied for some reason. This denial does not mean the process is finished. The business of insurance is just that, a business. Sometimes insurers use denials as a way to delay payments for services, which ultimately are reimbursed. Take a deep breath and then implement the plan listed below to pursue payment for services.

Appealing an Adverse Decision

Contact the case manager or claim manager and present the following questions:

- What was the reason for denial?
- Who made this decision?
  - Was it an MD?
  - Was the reviewer a specialist in the field for the services he/she reviewed?
- What is the appeals process?

Filing the Appeal

- Is additional information needed to review the appealed case?
- Involve the referring physician
  - Obtain a letter outlining the medical or behavioral need for music therapy
- Involve the client and/or family
  - Send them copies of all insurance company correspondence

Music Therapy
Reimbursement Best Practices

AMTA Operational Plan Reimbursement Initiative

AMTA's Strategic Plan is a dynamic document detailing the goals and objectives of the Association. Developed by the AMTA Board of Directors, with input from the AMTA National Office Staff, the Strategic Plan serves to direct the programs and activities of the Association. As this plan is operationalized and implemented, the Board of Directors evaluates, refines, revises, and expands the goals and objectives in order to fulfill and fully realize the mission of AMTA.

In its efforts to further the Association mission, the AMTA Board of Directors identified reimbursement as a priority within the existing association Strategic Plan. An extensive four-year operational plan (Appendix, page 81) was initiated in July 2001 to address this important topic. Development of this reimbursement best practices manual is one of the many tasks outlined within the operational plan. To date, several other tasks within the plan have also been completed. Work continues as we strive to achieve the remaining tasks, focused on four target groups of music therapists, insurance companies and government agencies, service providers, and consumers.

Survey Results

As part of the operational plan, the AMTA membership was surveyed to determine the level of reimbursement music therapists were receiving from third party-payers. The driving question was, "How many music therapists are receiving insurance reimbursement?" A web-based surveyed was distributed to 407 music therapists who indicated on the AMTA membership survey that they had received reimbursement for music therapy services. The AMTA member then completed the survey and emailed his or her answers. This was an efficient way to obtain information about reimbursement from the membership.

The questions were asked in an attempt to determine how much reimbursement music therapists were receiving and under what circumstances. One hundred and thirteen music therapists returned the survey and are included in the analysis. Forty-seven percent of the respondents had a bachelor's degree, 48% had a master's, and 5% had a doctoral degree. Fifty-one percent of the music therapists indicated that they had worked as a music therapist for 10 or more years; 9% indicated that they had worked less than 2 years. Ninety-five percent indicated that that they had board certification, and 30% indicated that they had an active private practice. Fifty-four percent described the community where they worked as suburban area.

When queried about receiving payment for services, 54% indicated that they had billed for music therapy services. The following table indicates the frequency with which music therapists or their organizations had received third-party reimbursement for music therapy services. Interestingly, some individuals indicated on the membership survey that they had received reimbursement for services, but on this survey they indicated they had never received reimbursement for music therapy services. The discrepancy could be the result of individuals changing jobs in which they no longer submit for reimbursement, or some respondents did not understand the terminology in the survey.

Reimbursement Frequency

		Frequency	Percentage	Valid Percentage	Cumulative Percentage
Valid	Never	42	37.2	37.2	37.2
	A little of the time	11	9.7	9.7	46.9
	Some of the time	12	10.6	10.6	57.5
	Most of the time	13	11.5	11.5	69.0
	All of the time	35	31.0	31.0	100.0
	Total	113	100.0	100.0	

Individuals who indicated they had never received reimbursement were eliminated from further analysis.

Nonparametric analyses indicated that there was no difference in reimbursement based on years of experience, education level, or credentialing. There was also no relationship between receiving reimbursement and years of experience, education level, or credentialing. The only relationship between reimbursement and characteristics of therapists was that individuals who actually applied for reimbursement were more likely to receive third-party payment than those individuals who did not apply.

The results of this survey indicate that some music therapists who are billing third-party payers are receiving reimbursement for music therapy. The data also indicate that the level of reimbursement for services is not driven by education level, years of experience, or credentialing. The only possible predictor from this data set that may determine reimbursement for music therapy is whether or not services were billed to a third-party payer.

Interview Results

The following information was gleaned from telephone interviews with 15 music therapists who indicated receiving reimbursement either all of the time or most of the time. Each music therapist provided valuable information about the various forms of payment/reimbursement that they received from different organizations. The information that they provided was compiled by combining the stories they told about their experiences with reimbursement. These experiences included both thoughts and details about the process that they underwent in order to provide music therapy. The information is organized by the mechanism of reimbursement and not patient population.

Medicare

The music therapists we spoke to who were receiving reimbursement/payment from Medicare were employed or contracted by an organization that billed Medicare for a per diem rate. Since we already know that Medicare provides coverage for music therapy in Partial Hospitalization Programs (PHP), this section describes a different example of music therapy coverage under a Medicare per diem rate, specifically in Hospice.

Hospice

Of the music therapists we interviewed, two specifically mentioned being reimbursed through Medicare for hospice services. Typically, music therapy services for hospice patients are paid for by the hospice organization's general fund. The organization receives Medicare funds for each individual being cared for by the organization. It is then the organization's responsibility to manage the funds to pay different healthcare providers. Therefore, unlike some of the other mechanisms for payment and reimbursement, there is not a pre-approval process per se for hospice work. The hospice regulates how the funds will be dispersed for rendered services.

The process of receiving payment for hospice was consistent between the two interviewees. Prior to services being provided, the music therapists presented inservices to the organization's case managers and administrators. During the inservices, the music therapists provided information about the use of music therapy in hospice, typical goals and interventions, and research results. Publications from AMTA such as the *What is Music Therapy?* brochure and *Music Therapy for Older Adults* were also distributed to the hospice team members and administration.

Since the hospice organizations regulate how their funds from Medicare reimbursement will be spent, the referral process and documentation requirements are different depending on the organization's standards of practice. The music therapists interviewed submitted an invoice detailing session times and mileage (unlike some other sources of payment, mileage is a reimbursable expense). Along with the invoice, the therapists also submitted an interdisciplinary note to document the client's progress toward treatment goals.

According to our interviews, payment for services can take approximately one month. Negotiating payment rates has not been a contentious issue. The music therapists suggested fees based on what other music therapists having approximately the same amount of experience and education in the area charge. The hospice organizations have accepted the payment requests without discussion.

Private Insurance Companies

Reimbursement from private insurance companies depends on the state or region. For instance, Blue Cross Blue Shield has reimbursed for music therapy services on the East coast, but has refused to reimburse for music therapy services in the Midwest. But there is one thing that is very clear: music therapists will not receive reimbursement for services if they don't attempt to gain pre-approval to provide services or submit bills for payment.

Initial referrals for services do not typically vary by reimbursement source. Therefore, there is some redundancy when discussing referral sources for music therapists. Referrals can come from caseworkers, nurses, speech pathologists, and even work rehabilitation programs. While the source of the referral may vary, one music therapist indicated that she does not do any insurance work without a written physician prescription for music therapy services. The prescription can lend some validation for the request for music therapy and can also help determine the therapy schedule. So if a referral comes from a parent or another healthcare professional, the music therapist in this case always seeks a prescription or order from the physician for music therapy services.

After a referral is made, the music therapist may speak directly with an insurance case manager. This is an opportunity to provide information about music therapy, including sending publications documenting the effects of music therapy with the relevant diagnoses or population. Music therapists have included AMTA fact sheets, research articles, popular press articles, certification information, a business card or brochure, and fee schedule. Once a therapist has been reimbursed from a particular company, subsequent reimbursement procedures are easier to negotiate. But the therapist should not assume that the caseworkers from the insurance company communicate with one another. Inservices to educate caseworkers from insurance companies may be beneficial.

Pre-approval can take two forms. After an individual is referred, the music therapist can obtain approval from an insurance caseworker to conduct an assessment. After the assessment, approval is granted via a letter from the insurance company stating that the music therapy is deemed medically necessary. The second option could include becoming a provider for an insurance company. For instance, in Washington state, there is a form called the Washington Practitioner's Application. It is a non-discipline specific form that inquires about the applicant's clinical information, license number, experiences, and references. It is a lengthy document, but it is filled out once and then submitted to various insurance companies to be a provider. With this process, it appears that applicants must provide evidence of an advanced degree and licensure in a related healthcare field in order to be considered as an approved provider.

Documentation requirements from insurance companies also vary. It was fairly consistent among our interviewees that monthly written reports accompanied invoices for payment. These reports provided information about medical and behavioral necessity, functional outcomes, and related treatment planning and goals. Very rarely have music therapists had to choose a CPT code for billing; the insurance companies assist the therapist in determining the most appropriate CPT code depending on the goals of therapy and the reason for referral. As an aside, these monthly reports can be sent to the physicians, treatment team, or guardians as long as there is a written release signed by the appropriate person.

In some cases, therapists stated that they bill the patient or guardian and then the patient or guardian takes responsibility to obtain reimbursement from the insurance company. For instance, in Massachusetts, a mother wanted music therapy for her child who was turning 4. She advocated for her child receiving reimbursement for music therapy services from their private insurance company. The music therapist billed the parents for the therapy services. The mother then submitted claim forms to the insurance company to receive payment for services.

Music therapists who are submitting invoices to private insurance companies generally set their rates based on other allied health profession rates (e.g., occupational therapists, physical therapists). Whatever is billed, the insurance company may pay only a percentage of what is billed, expecting the patient to pay the balance of the bill. Turn-around time for payment can vary depending on the level of expertise of the music therapist doing the billing. One of the interviewees indicated that initially the turn-around time to receive reimbursement was 2–3 months, but as she became more adept, the billing cycle changed to monthly.

There can be multiple opportunities for collaboration within the auspice of insurance reimbursement. We have reports of music therapists receiving courtesy updates about their patients from the physicians and other healthcare providers. Additionally, the insurance caseworkers may be involved in team meetings that occur on a regular basis, monthly or quarterly.

Workers' Compensation

The music therapists interviewed from Texas, Ohio, and Alabama indicated they were receiving some funds from private companies for workers' compensation claims. It is separated out from private insurance because there was a distinct subset of music therapists who were receiving reimbursement from private insurance companies for workers' compensation claims.

The initial contact or referral for workers' compensation rehabilitation usually came from a caseworker and concerned patients with traumatic brain injuries. This caseworker would often obtain a physician prescription for music therapy services. The prescriptions can be fairly specific. One physician in particular indicated in his dictations that he was referring a patient for music therapy because of the documented research results from the literature. This particular physician wrote for music therapy two to three times per week for four months.

The pre-approval process may take a while and the caseworker can work as an advocate to the insurance company to help facilitate the process of reimbursement. We have one report of the pre-approval process taking one year before finally receiving approval. Documentation the music therapists have provided to facilitate approval have included the AMTA fact sheets, brochures, business cards, and professional licensure or certification. Once approval was given, it was for a finite amount of time, such as three months. There was then a reassessment process before approval for further therapy.

Claims for payment include therapist-created invoices along with the workers' compensation claim forms. As with other private insurance claim information, the insurance companies assisted the music therapist in determining the appropriate CPT code to use in the reimbursement process. Monthly reports documenting medical necessity, including outcomes with goals and progression toward goals, were included with the claims for payment. The submission of reports documenting behavioral necessity, functional outcomes, and treatment plan goals were consistent from interview to interview. Additionally, one therapist indicated that she provided evidence of transferring the skills learned in therapy to the community setting.

As stated previously, therapists generally turn in monthly invoices; turn-around time for payment can vary from 30–45 days. Therapists receiving reimbursement for services have used the AMTA Descriptive Statistical Profile to help in determining and negotiating fees. There were no indications that insurance companies were negotiating about rates; the companies usually reimbursed the therapist what was quoted.

Departments of Social & Health Services (Federal or State Dollars)

First Steps (Early Intervention)

First Steps is a state-run program for children 0–3 years of age. Because it is a state program that manages federal dollars, programs vary from state to state. For instance, in Massachusetts, music therapists who work with Early Intervention children are paid as employees of the Department of Public Health; in other states, providers are contracted. Some Early Intervention programs are reluctant to pay for music therapy services. However, parents and other providers can be effective advocates for music therapy services. In one case, a pediatric physical therapist told a First Steps caseworker that a child needed music therapy services. This precipitated the use of music therapy for that particular child and opened the door for further referrals for children.

Referral sources for music therapy in early intervention can come from multiple sources. Other Early Intervention providers, parents, and healthcare professionals can be advocates for music therapy services. Educating Early Intervention administration about research results and providing a bibliography of research with the AMTA fact sheets and the difference between music education and music therapy can also be helpful in starting the process of music therapy reimbursement. The important issue in advocating for music therapy services within Early Intervention is understanding the language that the Early Intervention providers use and any special requirements for training. For instance, in Indiana, even with board certification, a music therapist would have to obtain certification from the First Steps program in Indiana. This requires additional hours of education and supervision from another professional. One therapist in Tennessee indicated that she needed to obtain status as an "S" corporation prior to receiving any contracts from the state Early Intervention program. Incorporation gave her a level of credibility that she didn't have as a sole proprietor.

When beginning a contract with the Early Intervention program, it is helpful to obtain a contract stating what the fee will be prior to providing services. This step has resulted in assuring minimal problems in receiving payment. The payment schedule reported by the music therapists who provide services for Early Intervention ranged from 21–30 days.

Once a referral is made and the therapist starts providing services to the child, clear and concise progress notes can provide a means to communicate with the case manager and treatment team. The level of detail in progress notes varied from therapist to therapist. The most detailed notes included a task analysis of goals and objectives for each client. These task analyses were in a spreadsheet for each client. Documentation of behaviors targeted in each objective was then recorded on the spreadsheet, leading to an easy way to graph the child's progress. A narrative describing the data on the spreadsheet accompanied the invoice at the end of the billing cycle. The narrative included information about functional outcomes, behavioral outcomes, and pre-educational goals. Many of these reports were written on the therapist's own letterhead, but there may be a requirement to use forms from the Early Intervention program.

Family Support Opportunity

There are some funds that each state or local government disperses as discretionary money to individual families with children with development delays. A specific dollar amount is provided to the family for equipment or services that aren't usually covered by Medicaid waiver funds. These discretionary monies are available in Ohio, Washington, Illinois, and Wisconsin. The family is responsible for managing the funds and keeping track of the balance available. The music therapists who were interviewed indicated that this is an easy way for families to pay for music therapy services.

Medicaid

Partial Hospitalization

In Ohio, a Partial Hospitalization Program covers music therapy in the Medicaid per diem rate. The children, 8–18 years of age, are in the program for three hours a day and attend groups such as psychotherapy and music therapy. Typical diagnoses include Attention Deficit-Hyperactivity, Conduct Disorder, and Post Traumatic Stress. Most of the kids have been either abused or neglected. Some of the children are assigned to the program through the courts after being charged with sexual offenses. Everybody in the program receives music therapy. There is no specific physician order for services.

Documentation for Partial Hospitalization is fastidious. The music therapist documents every day. Documentation for the Partial Hospitalization Program includes time logs and progress notes. The logs include the time and number of participants within each music therapy session. Goals and objectives that the primary therapist has established for each child are also included in the logs. The music therapist circles the goals that were worked on within the therapy session and indicates the child's level of involvement in the therapy session. The child's level of involvement in the therapy must be established through documentation of observable behaviors in order for the facility to receive reimbursement.

Medicaid Waiver

States throughout the country have started to include music therapy as a reimbursable service within the Medicaid waver. Since the Medicaid waiver is federal dollars administrated by the state, the requirements for obtaining reimbursement vary from state to state. Some states require the music therapist to obtain a provider number. Texas does not require music therapists to obtain provider status. This is most likely due to the fact that billing and services are managed through an organization. If the therapist does not have a provider number, he or she may need to provide proof of credentials.

A parent will often advocate for the child who has a developmental disability to receive music therapy services within the Medicaid waiver program. If music therapists advocate for music therapy services, it is often seen as self-serving. So music therapists can assist parents in advocating for their own child by giving them the information about music therapy to share with the caseworker.

Music therapists who receive reimbursement through the Medicaid waiver talk mostly about the documentation that is needed to obtain reimbursement. The process for referral and assessment are not unfamiliar processes. After parents indicate that they want to receive music therapy services for their child, a caseworker often gets involved to facilitate the beginning of services and requests an assessment.

When the music therapist provides an assessment, treatment goals and objectives should include targeting functional outcomes. Assessment and weekly progress notes can be mailed in to the state. Subsequent updates, quarterly or yearly, may include a team meeting in which the music therapist can be involved.

Billing for services may require the music therapist to fill out a form 3625 to document the hour units of service. Music therapists have told us that they sometimes copy the form unto their own letterhead, or include their own invoice with the state form. Medicaid requirements and procedures vary from state to state. Some states allow billing for travel and documentation time; other states allow the therapist to bill only for direct client contact hours. Music therapists who want to be reimbursed through the Medicaid waiver system will need to become familiar with their own state's regulations.

Best Practice Essential Components

Medicare

Hospice

- Music therapy services for hospice patients are generally paid for by the hospice organization's general fund.
- Therapists present inservices to the organization's case managers and administrators and provide published information about the use of music therapy in hospice, typical goals and interventions, and research results.
- Music therapists submit invoices detailing session times and mileage, and interdisciplinary notes to document the client's progress toward treatment goals.

Private Insurance Companies

- Referrals can come from caseworkers, nurses, speech pathologists, guardians, and even work rehabilitation programs.
- Clinicians should obtain a written physician prescription for music therapy services.
- Therapists educate the insurance case manager about music therapy and send publications and research documenting the effects of music therapy with the relevant diagnoses or population.
- Therapists send monthly written reports with invoices providing information about medical and behavioral necessity, functional outcomes, and related treatment planning and goals.

Workers' Compensation

- The initial contact or referral for workers' compensation for rehabilitation usually comes from a caseworker.
- Clinicians should obtain a physician prescription for music therapy services.
- The caseworker can work as an advocate to the insurance company to help facilitate the process of reimbursement.
- Therapists submit monthly reports documenting medical necessity, including outcomes with goals and progression toward goals, which are then included with the claims for payment.

Departments of Social & Health Services (Federal or State Dollars)

First Steps (Early Intervention)

- Parents and other providers can be effective advocates for music therapy services.
- Educating Early Intervention administrators can be helpful in starting the process of music therapy reimbursement.
- Clinicians should understand the language that the Early Intervention providers use and should know about any special requirements for training.
- Clear and concise progress notes can provide a means to communicate with the case manager and treatment team.

Family Support Opportunity

- A specific dollar amount is provided to the family for equipment or services that are not usually covered by Medicaid waiver funds.
- The family is responsible for managing the funds and keeping track of the balance available.

Medicaid

Partial Hospitalization

- Music therapy services are covered under a per diem rate.
- Detailed daily documentation is required, including time logs and progress notes.
- Goals and objectives for each participant must be clear.
- The participants' levels of involvement must be established through documentation of observable behaviors.

Medicaid Waivers

- Some states require the music therapist to obtain a provider number.
- Parents will often advocate for their children who have developmental disabilities to receive music therapy services within the Medicaid waiver program.
- When the music therapist provides an assessment, treatment goals and objectives should include targeting functional outcomes.
- Music therapists who want to be reimbursed through the Medicaid waiver system need to become familiar with their own state's regulations.

Resources and Tools:
Forms, Marketing, and Research

Sample Forms

- Music Therapy Treatment Prior Approval Form
- Assignment of Benefits/Release of Medical Information
- Approval Confirmation Letter Template
- Prior Approval Letter Template
- Billing/Claim Submission Worksheet
- CMS 1500 Billing Form

MUSIC THERAPY TREATMENT PRIOR APPROVAL FORM

Date referred: _____   Referred by: _____

Patient name: _____   DOB: ____/____/____

Date of Injury: ____/____/____   Diagnosis: _____

Plan/Employer Group name: _____   Plan/Policy Number: _____

Health Plan/Insurance Company Name: _____

Member (Insured) name: _____ Member ID: _____

Patient's relationship to the member: _____ Plan type: Indemnity   PPO   POS   HMO
                                                                                    (circle one)

Benefits Verification

Phone number: (____) ____-_____   Spoke with: _____

Is the patient eligible for benefits?   ❑ Y   ❑ N

Is there a benefit for music therapy?   ❑ Y   ❑ N

Benefits: _____

Plan Requirements

Does this plan require PCP approval?   ❑ Y   ❑ N

PCP name: _____

PCP phone number: (____) ____-_____

PCP address: _____

City: _____   State: _____   Zip: _____

Network Requirement?   ❑ Y   ❑ N   Name of Network: _____

Prior Approval Request

Date contacted: _____   Case Manager Name: _____

Case Manager's phone number: (____) ____-_____

Authorization number: _____

Forward proposed care plan to: _____

City: _____   State: _____   Zip: _____

Will they be forwarding a written confirmation or determination?   ❑ Y   ❑ N

Billing/Claim Information

Claims should be submitted to:

Care Manager? _____   Claims Manager? _____

Address: _____

City: _____   State: _____   Zip: _____

Assignment of Benefits/
Release of Medical Information

With my signature below I hereby authorize all of my insurance companies to make payment directly to **YOUR NAME HERE**. This assignment will remain in effect until revoked by me in writing. I understand that I am financially responsible for all charges whether or not paid by said insurance company. I authorize the release of any medical information necessary to process these claims.

Patient Signature: _____

Date: _____

Approval Confirmation Letter Template

DATE

CARE MANAGER NAME _OR_ **MEDICAL REVIEW DEPARTMENT CONTACT**
MEDICAL REVIEW DEPARTMENT
NAME OF INSURANCE COMPANY/HEALTH PLAN
ADDRESS

Re: **Patient Name**   **Plan/Policy Number**
        Date of Birth   **Group Name (Employer Group), if applicable**
        Member ID

Dear **CONTACT NAME:**

It was a pleasure speaking with you regarding **PATIENT NAME** and **HEALTH PLAN/INSURANCE COMPANY'S** case management program. This letter is a confirmation of our conversation on **DATE** where it was agreed that the following services that I will be providing are approved at the rates outlined below:

DATE(S) OF SERVICE   SERVICE FREQUENCY   RATE

These services were also approved by **PRIMARY CARE OR REFERRING PHYSICIAN NAME HERE**.

Claims for these services should be forwarded to the following location:

CASE MANAGER OR CLAIM MANAGER NAME
HEALTH PLAN/INSURANCE COMPANY NAME
ADDRESS

As we discussed, I will be providing clinical updates to you **FREQUENCY HERE**. Should you have questions regarding the treatment or the patient's progress, please feel free to contact me.

Please do not hesitate to contact me at **YOUR PHONE NUMBER HERE** if your understanding of this agreement differs.

Sincerely,

YOUR NAME
ORGANIZATION, IF APPLICABLE
ADDRESS, PHONE, FAX

Cc: **THE PATIENT**

Prior Approval Letter Template

DATE

MEDICAL REVIEW DEPARTMENT
NAME OF CONTACT, IF APPLICABLE
NAME OF INSURANCE COMPANY/HEALTH PLAN
ADDRESS

Re: **Patient Name**
     Date of Birth
     Member ID
     Plan/Policy Number
     Group Name (Employer Group), if applicable

Dear Medical Reviewer:

I am writing on behalf of my patient, **NAME HERE**, to request a prior approval for **SERVICES/THERAPY HERE** which includes **CPT CODES HERE** for **ICD-9 CODES HERE** for **NUMBER OF TREATMENTS** from **DATE** to **DATE.**

The patient was referred to me by **REFERRING PHYSICIAN NAME HERE** on **REFERRAL DATE** to treat **LIST DEFICITS HERE** at **OUTPATIENT FACILITY NAME HERE, IF APPLICABLE**. The goal(s) of treatment are:

> **Measurable goals should be listed here in a clear and concise manner.**

I have attached a copy of the initial evaluation for treatment with this request. Please feel free to contact me for additional information or with questions you may have.

As this patient has not yet started treatment, we are anxious to receive a decision within **DAYS** ensuring that delays in treatment are avoided and the patient can continue to progress.

Thanking you in advance for your timely response,

YOUR NAME
ORGANIZATION, IF APPLICABLE
ADDRESS
PHONE
FAX

Cc: **THE PATIENT**
     THE REFERRING PHYSICIAN

MUSIC THERAPY
BILLING/CLAIM SUBMISSION WORKSHEET

Date Referred: _____ Referred By: _____

Patient Name: _____

Street Address: _____ City: _____ State: _____

Zip: _____ Phone: _____

Patient's DOB: _____ Patient's Relationship to Insured member: _____

Insured Member Name: _____

Street Address: _____ City: _____ State: _____

Zip: _____ Phone: _____

Plan/Policy Number: _____ Member ID: _____

Health Plan/Insurance Company Name: _____

Plan/Employer Group Name: _____

Plan Type: Indemnity   PPO   POS   HMO   (circle one)

Primary Care Physician: _____

PCP Phone: _____   Referral Received: Y   N

Is the member employed? Y or N   Auto Accident? Y or N Other Accident? Y or N

Is there another health benefit plan that the patient is covered under?   Y or N

If yes:

Plan/Policy Number: _____ Member ID: _____

Health Plan/Insurance Company Name: _____

Plan/Employer Group Name: _____

Plan Type: Indemnity   PPO   POS   HMO   (circle one)

Diagnoses:

      Primary (main event—e.g., stroke) _____

      Secondary (why you are treating—e.g., aphasia) _____

Care Manager/Claim Manager: _____

Phone: _____

Approval obtained from: _____

Date: _____ Confirmed in writing on: _____

Dates of Service: _____

_____

Approved Procedure (CPT) Codes: _____

Rates Negotiated: _____

Claims should be sent to:

Care Manager: _____ Claims Manager: _____

Address: _____ PO Box: _____

City: _____ State: _____ Zip:_____

_____

Special Instructions:

Attachments to Claim?

Update Requirements?

PLEASE
DO NOT
STAPLE
IN THIS
AREA

← CARRIER

| | PICA | | | **HEALTH INSURANCE CLAIM FORM** | PICA | | |

| 1. MEDICARE | MEDICAID | CHAMPUS | CHAMPVA | GROUP HEALTH PLAN (SSN or ID) | FECA BLK LUNG (SSN) | OTHER | 1a. INSURED'S I.D. NUMBER (FOR PROGRAM IN ITEM 1) |
| (Medicare #) | (Medicaid #) | (Sponsor's SSN) | (VA File #) | | | (ID) | |

2. PATIENT'S NAME (Last Name, First Name, Middle Initial)

3. PATIENT'S BIRTH DATE MM DD YY   SEX M   F

4. INSURED'S NAME (Last Name, First Name, Middle Initial)

5. PATIENT'S ADDRESS (No., Street)

6. PATIENT RELATIONSHIP TO INSURED Self Spouse Child Other

7. INSURED'S ADDRESS (No., Street)

CITY   STATE

8. PATIENT STATUS Single Married Other

Employed Full-Time Student Part-Time Student

CITY   STATE

ZIP CODE   TELEPHONE (Include Area Code) ( )

ZIP CODE   TELEPHONE (INCLUDE AREA CODE) ( )

9. OTHER INSURED'S NAME (Last Name, First Name, Middle Initial)

10. IS PATIENT'S CONDITION RELATED TO:

11. INSURED'S POLICY GROUP OR FECA NUMBER

a. OTHER INSURED'S POLICY OR GROUP NUMBER

a. EMPLOYMENT? (CURRENT OR PREVIOUS) YES NO

a. INSURED'S DATE OF BIRTH MM DD YY   SEX M F

b. OTHER INSURED'S DATE OF BIRTH MM DD YY SEX M F

b. AUTO ACCIDENT? PLACE (State) YES NO

b. EMPLOYER'S NAME OR SCHOOL NAME

c. EMPLOYER'S NAME OR SCHOOL NAME

c. OTHER ACCIDENT? YES NO

c. INSURANCE PLAN NAME OR PROGRAM NAME

d. INSURANCE PLAN NAME OR PROGRAM NAME

10d. RESERVED FOR LOCAL USE

d. IS THERE ANOTHER HEALTH BENEFIT PLAN? YES NO If yes, return to and complete item 9 a-d.

READ BACK OF FORM BEFORE COMPLETING & SIGNING THIS FORM.

12. PATIENT'S OR AUTHORIZED PERSON'S SIGNATURE I authorize the release of any medical or other information necessary to process this claim. I also request payment of government benefits either to myself or to the party who accepts assignment below.

SIGNED _____ DATE _____

13. INSURED'S OR AUTHORIZED PERSON'S SIGNATURE I authorize payment of medical benefits to the undersigned physician or supplier for services described below.

SIGNED _____

14. DATE OF CURRENT: MM DD YY ILLNESS (First symptom) OR INJURY (Accident) OR PREGNANCY(LMP)

15. IF PATIENT HAS HAD SAME OR SIMILAR ILLNESS. GIVE FIRST DATE MM DD YY

16. DATES PATIENT UNABLE TO WORK IN CURRENT OCCUPATION FROM MM DD YY TO MM DD YY

17. NAME OF REFERRING PHYSICIAN OR OTHER SOURCE

17a. I.D. NUMBER OF REFERRING PHYSICIAN

18. HOSPITALIZATION DATES RELATED TO CURRENT SERVICES FROM MM DD YY TO MM DD YY

19. RESERVED FOR LOCAL USE

20. OUTSIDE LAB? YES NO $ CHARGES

21. DIAGNOSIS OR NATURE OF ILLNESS OR INJURY. (RELATE ITEMS 1,2,3 OR 4 TO ITEM 24E BY LINE)

1. |___.__| 3. |___.__|

2. |___.__| 4. |___.__|

22. MEDICAID RESUBMISSION CODE   ORIGINAL REF. NO.

23. PRIOR AUTHORIZATION NUMBER

24. A DATE(S) OF SERVICE From / To MM DD YY MM DD YY	B Place of Service	C Type of Service	D PROCEDURES, SERVICES, OR SUPPLIES (Explain Unusual Circumstances) CPT/HCPCS MODIFIER	E DIAGNOSIS CODE	F $ CHARGES	G DAYS OR UNITS	H EPSDT Family Plan	I EMG	J COB	K RESERVED FOR LOCAL USE
1										
2										
3										
4										
5										
6										

25. FEDERAL TAX I.D. NUMBER SSN EIN

26. PATIENT'S ACCOUNT NO.

27. ACCEPT ASSIGNMENT? (For govt. claims, see back) YES NO

28. TOTAL CHARGE $

29. AMOUNT PAID $

30. BALANCE DUE $

31. SIGNATURE OF PHYSICIAN OR SUPPLIER INCLUDING DEGREES OR CREDENTIALS (I certify that the statements on the reverse apply to this bill and are made a part thereof.)

SIGNED _____ DATE _____

32. NAME AND ADDRESS OF FACILITY WHERE SERVICES WERE RENDERED (If other than home or office)

33. PHYSICIAN'S, SUPPLIER'S BILLING NAME, ADDRESS, ZIP CODE & PHONE #

PIN#   GRP#

(APPROVED BY AMA COUNCIL ON MEDICAL SERVICE 8/88)   **PLEASE PRINT OR TYPE**   APPROVED OMB-0938-0008 FORM CMS-1500 (12-90), FORM RRB-1500, APPROVED OMB-1215-0055 FORM OWCP-1500, APPROVED OMB-0720-0001 (CHAMPUS)

PATIENT AND INSURED INFORMATION →   PHYSICIAN OR SUPPLIER INFORMATION →

BECAUSE THIS FORM IS USED BY VARIOUS GOVERNMENT AND PRIVATE HEALTH PROGRAMS, SEE SEPARATE INSTRUCTIONS ISSUED BY APPLICABLE PROGRAMS.

NOTICE: Any person who knowingly files a statement of claim containing any misrepresentation or any false, incomplete or misleading information may be guilty of a criminal act punishable under law and may be subject to civil penalties.

REFERS TO GOVERNMENT PROGRAMS ONLY

MEDICARE AND CHAMPUS PAYMENTS: A patient's signature requests that payment be made and authorizes release of any information necessary to process the claim and certifies that the information provided in Blocks 1 through 12 is true, accurate and complete. In the case of a Medicare claim, the patient's signature authorizes any entity to release to Medicare medical and nonmedical information, including employment status, and whether the person has employer group health insurance, liability, no-fault, worker's compensation or other insurance which is responsible to pay for the services for which the Medicare claim is made. See 42 CFR 411.24(a). If item 9 is completed, the patient's signature authorizes release of the information to the health plan or agency shown. In Medicare assigned or CHAMPUS participation cases, the physician agrees to accept the charge determination of the Medicare carrier or CHAMPUS fiscal intermediary as the full charge, and the patient is responsible only for the deductible, coinsurance and noncovered services. Coinsurance and the deductible are based upon the charge determination of the Medicare carrier or CHAMPUS fiscal intermediary if this is less than the charge submitted. CHAMPUS is not a health insurance program but makes payment for health benefits provided through certain affiliations with the Uniformed Services. Information on the patient's sponsor should be provided in those items captioned in "Insured"; i.e., items 1a, 4, 6, 7, 9, and 11.

BLACK LUNG AND FECA CLAIMS

The provider agrees to accept the amount paid by the Government as payment in full. See Black Lung and FECA instructions regarding required procedure and diagnosis coding systems.

SIGNATURE OF PHYSICIAN OR SUPPLIER (MEDICARE, CHAMPUS, FECA AND BLACK LUNG)

I certify that the services shown on this form were medically indicated and necessary for the health of the patient and were personally furnished by me or were furnished incident to my professional service by my employee under my immediate personal supervision, except as otherwise expressly permitted by Medicare or CHAMPUS regulations.

For services to be considered as "incident" to a physician's professional service, 1) they must be rendered under the physician's immediate personal supervision by his/her employee, 2) they must be an integral, although incidental part of a covered physician's service, 3) they must be of kinds commonly furnished in physician's offices, and 4) the services of nonphysicians must be included on the physician's bills.

For CHAMPUS claims, I further certify that I (or any employee) who rendered services am not an active duty member of the Uniformed Services or a civilian employee of the United States Government or a contract employee of the United States Government, either civilian or military (refer to 5 USC 5536). For Black-Lung claims, I further certify that the services performed were for a Black Lung-related disorder.

No Part B Medicare benefits may be paid unless this form is received as required by existing law and regulations (42 CFR 424.32).

NOTICE: Any one who misrepresents or falsifies essential information to receive payment from Federal funds requested by this form may upon conviction be subject to fine and imprisonment under applicable Federal laws.

NOTICE TO PATIENT ABOUT THE COLLECTION AND USE OF MEDICARE, CHAMPUS, FECA, AND BLACK LUNG INFORMATION
(PRIVACY ACT STATEMENT)

We are authorized by CMS, CHAMPUS and OWCP to ask you for information needed in the administration of the Medicare, CHAMPUS, FECA, and Black Lung programs. Authority to collect information is in section 205(a), 1862, 1872 and 1874 of the Social Security Act as amended, 42 CFR 411.24(a) and 424.5(a) (6), and 44 USC 3101;41 CFR 101 et seq and 10 USC 1079 and 1086; 5 USC 8101 et seq; and 30 USC 901 et seq; 38 USC 613; E.O. 9397.

The information we obtain to complete claims under these programs is used to identify you and to determine your eligibility. It is also used to decide if the services and supplies you received are covered by these programs and to insure that proper payment is made.

The information may also be given to other providers of services, carriers, intermediaries, medical review boards, health plans, and other organizations or Federal agencies, for the effective administration of Federal provisions that require other third parties payers to pay primary to Federal program, and as otherwise necessary to administer these programs. For example, it may be necessary to disclose information about the benefits you have used to a hospital or doctor. Additional disclosures are made through routine uses for information contained in systems of records.

FOR MEDICARE CLAIMS: See the notice modifying system No. 09-70-0501, titled, 'Carrier Medicare Claims Record,' published in the Federal Register, Vol. 55 No. 177, page 37549, Wed. Sept. 12, 1990, or as updated and republished.

FOR OWCP CLAIMS: Department of Labor, Privacy Act of 1974, "Republication of Notice of Systems of Records," Federal Register Vol. 55 No. 40, Wed Feb. 28, 1990, See ESA-5, ESA-6, ESA-12, ESA-13, ESA-30, or as updated and republished.

FOR CHAMPUS CLAIMS: PRINCIPLE PURPOSE(S): To evaluate eligibility for medical care provided by civilian sources and to issue payment upon establishment of eligibility and determination that the services/supplies received are authorized by law.

ROUTINE USE(S): Information from claims and related documents may be given to the Dept. of Veterans Affairs, the Dept. of Health and Human Services and/or the Dept. of Transportation consistent with their statutory administrative responsibilities under CHAMPUS/CHAMPVA; to the Dept. of Justice for representation of the Secretary of Defense in civil actions; to the Internal Revenue Service, private collection agencies, and consumer reporting agencies in connection with recoupment claims; and to Congressional Offices in response to inquiries made at the request of the person to whom a record pertains. Appropriate disclosures may be made to other federal, state, local, foreign government agencies, private business entities, and individual providers of care, on matters relating to entitlement, claims adjudication, fraud, program abuse, utilization review, quality assurance, peer review, program integrity, third-party liability, coordination of benefits, and civil and criminal litigation related to the operation of CHAMPUS.

DISCLOSURES: Voluntary; however, failure to provide information will result in delay in payment or may result in denial of claim. With the one exception discussed below, there are no penalties under these programs for refusing to supply information. However, failure to furnish information regarding the medical services rendered or the amount charged would prevent payment of claims under these programs. Failure to furnish any other information, such as name or claim number, would delay payment of the claim. Failure to provide medical information under FECA could be deemed an obstruction.

It is mandatory that you tell us if you know that another party is responsible for paying for your treatment. Section 1128B of the Social Security Act and 31 USC 3801-3812 provide penalties for withholding this information.

You should be aware that P.L. 100-503, the "Computer Matching and Privacy Protection Act of 1988", permits the government to verify information by way of computer matches.

MEDICAID PAYMENTS (PROVIDER CERTIFICATION)

I hereby agree to keep such records as are necessary to disclose fully the extent of services provided to individuals under the State's Title XIX plan and to furnish information regarding any payments claimed for providing such services as the State Agency or Dept. of Health and Humans Services may request.

I further agree to accept, as payment in full, the amount paid by the Medicaid program for those claims submitted for payment under that program, with the exception of authorized deductible, coinsurance, co-payment or similar cost-sharing charge.

SIGNATURE OF PHYSICIAN (OR SUPPLIER): I certify that the services listed above were medically indicated and necessary to the health of this patient and were personally furnished by me or my employee under my personal direction.

NOTICE: This is to certify that the foregoing information is true, accurate and complete. I understand that payment and satisfaction of this claim will be from Federal and State funds, and that any false claims, statements, or documents, or concealment of a material fact, may be prosecuted under applicable Federal or State laws.

According to the Paperwork Reduction Act of 1995, no persons are required to respond to a collection of information unless it displays a valid OMB control number. The valid OMB control number for this information collection is 0938-0008. The time required to complete this information collection is estimated to average 10 minutes per response, including the time to review instructions, search existing data resources, gather the data needed, and complete and review the information collection. If you have any comments concerning the accuracy of the time estimate(s) or suggestions for improving this form, please write to: CMS, N2-14-26, 7500 Security Boulevard, Baltimore, Maryland 21244-1850.

Marketing

- Advocating for Music Therapy Services
- AMTA Fact Sheet
- AMTA Reimbursement Facts

Advocating for Music Therapy Services

All music therapists have skills in advocacy, even if they don't realize it. For example, when explaining to your family and friends about your career choice, when seeking employment, or when marketing a new private practice, you are in a sense "advocating" for music therapy. An advocate is defined as, "one that argues for a cause; a supporter or defender" or, "one that pleads in another's behalf" (American Heritage Dictionary, 2000).

Although sometimes we may feel like the need to "plead" occurs too often, every time you speak up for music therapy and its benefits, you are acting as an advocate for the profession. In many situations, the ability to support and defend is not difficult to learn, and in some individuals, the ability seems to develop naturally. This section will discuss taking that ability to the next level and utilizing it to increase access to services by influencing reimbursement decisions.

Most advocacy efforts can be divided into two categories: advocacy completed with members of Congress, with accrediting agencies, or with insurance company national representatives falls into a macro type of intervention—addressing the issue on a national or large-scale level. Advocacy completed with individual facilities, individual insurance company case managers, or families and clients falls into a micro type of intervention—addressing the issue on a smaller and more detailed level. Both types of advocacy are critical in the quest for successful reimbursement of music therapy.

Over the years, members of the association have worked together to establish mechanisms that approach reimbursement on the national level. Initially, a Reimbursement Task Force volunteered countless hours to assist members seeking coverage for interventions. In 2003, a new Reimbursement Standing Committee has been established for the first time, pushing this topic to the forefront of professional issues alongside government relations, research, and standards of clinical practice.

The "big picture" agenda continues pursuit of national recognition through increasing the percentage of reimbursed music therapy services. At the same, however, the efforts conducted on the local and single case level are what provide necessary background support for the national agenda. Each time a music therapist successfully receives third-party reimbursement for recommended services, it ultimately has a positive impact on national advocacy efforts.

What Can I Do to Advocate for Music Therapy?

As noted above, advocacy occurs on many levels and can influence many situations. For the issue of furthering reimbursement success, one needs to review the following basic questions:

1) WHO needs this information?
2) WHAT should I do about this issue?
3) WHEN should I advocate for music therapy?
4) WHERE should advocacy take place?
5) WHY should I advocate and why is this important to my practice as a music therapist?

WHO

Depending upon your employment situation, the list of individuals who could benefit from more information about music therapy can be quite extensive. Keep in mind these individuals might also be able to help you in your efforts to increase access through increased reimbursement.

- Facility Billing Department
- Facility Marketing Department
- Facility Administrators
- Insurance Company Representatives—Case Managers, Claim Managers, Utilization Review Directors
- Physicians and other Health Care Providers
- Corporations—Human Resources Director, Benefits Manager
- City, County, and State Agencies that address health care issues
- Consumers
- Music Industry

WHAT

Schedule a meeting with someone from the above list, stating that you would like to provide information about music therapy and the benefits available to (fill in the facility, population, diagnosis, or location being approached). Prior to the meeting, review these recommended steps:

- Educate yourself about the perspective and goals of the person(s) with whom you are meeting.
- Be prepared with specific goals that you want to accomplish during the meeting.
- Know the needs of the potential or established clients.
- Gather persuasive materials, such as research information, credential information from CBMT, and PR materials geared to the population.
- Have current copies of your resume, references, and proof of certification.
- Be prepared to discuss examples of successful music therapy reimbursement (see AMTA Reimbursement Facts, pp. 62–63).

During the actual meeting, consider these key steps:

- Give a brief introduction about yourself, music therapy, AMTA, and why you chose to meet with them.
- Explain what you do in music therapy and the clients you serve.
- Explain why you believe music therapy is a viable healthcare service.
- Present an extensive description of music therapy, its applications, and supportive research (see pp. 65–78). Utilize visuals when possible (videos, PowerPoint, brochures). Depending on situation, offer a live demonstration or experiential presentation.
- Emphasize how music therapy addresses clients' "functional outcomes."
- Answer questions and address concerns—indicate you will "get back to them" if you are unable to provide the information they request.
- Ask when would be a good time to follow up with them to continue the discussion about music therapy and the development of a possible working relationship.
- Thank them for their time.

WHEN

It is important to consider "timing" when advocating for music therapy. Although you will not know the details about a healthcare facility's financial situation, be conscious of budget concerns and recognize when marketing music therapy might be the cost-effective treatment your listener is seeking. This holds true whether your audience is a corporation representative, an insurance company case manager, a physician or related professional, or an individual client. If the interest is there but the timing is not right, offer to continue communication and mark your calendar to follow up in 6–12 months. Clinicians often discover their best source of referrals is an individual who was impressed by their advocacy efforts.

WHERE

Opportunities for advocacy can sometimes occur when you least expect it! Don't pass up a chance to advocate for music therapy, no matter what the setting. Consider some real-life scenarios:

Waiting in line at the supermarket, you strike up a conversation with the woman behind you. She states she is purchasing items for a party for residents in the nursing home where she works. You indicate you work as a music therapist and she states she would love to have a music therapist provide services to the residents. She invites you to contact the facility to discuss this option further and requests information on how the facility could cover your expenses.

Riding the train home, you start a conversation with the woman sitting next to you. She states she works as a clinical review manager for a major health insurance company. You state you are a music therapist and provide details about your work. She seems aware of the profession and asks detailed questions about required credentials and recognition by JCAHO. You ask if she would be willing to meet for lunch sometime to discuss how her company makes reimbursement decisions, as you are interested in learning how your clients can more easily access possible benefits for music therapy.

Obviously your advocacy does not always have to be a formal presentation. Sometimes you can make a positive impression during a simple and brief encounter. Take advantage of opportunities as they arise and discipline yourself to follow through with more detailed marketing tools as soon as possible.

WHY

It may seem redundant to review the why behind advocacy, but because of the potential outcomes, it is worth special attention. For many years, music therapists have been hired by facilities, either on a full- or part-time basis, and in some cases, the therapists have been able to work in that one facility for the majority of their careers. In recent years, however, with changes in the healthcare industry and a shift in employment trends, more and more music therapists find themselves working in consultant positions for several facilities or in their own private practice. When clinicians do work full-time with one employer, many have been approached for assistance in exploring reimbursement options.

Understanding the basics about reimbursement is essential regardless of the employment setting and situation. Whether justifying the cost effectiveness in a Medicare PPS system, establishing eligibility under Medicaid, or documenting medical necessity under private insurance, all music therapists must learn how to advocate for the inclusion of services and learn about possible reimbursement sources within their work environment.

Taking responsibility for this level of advocacy can be very motivating. Once you realize you have the ability to influence whether clients who need music therapy are able to access music therapy, the role of advocate takes on a new meaning. Instead of "pleading" you are "supporting"; instead of "defending," you are promoting—promoting the use of a treatment you know is viable. Take the opportunity to market music therapy with potential payers and promote increased access through increased reimbursement.

MUSIC THERAPY MAKES A DIFFERENCE

FACT SHEET

Music Therapy is an established health profession in which music is used within a therapeutic relationship to address physical, emotional, cognitive, and social needs of individuals of all ages. Music therapists use both instrumental and vocal music strategies to facilitate changes that are non-musical in nature. After assessment of the strengths and needs of each client, qualified music therapists provide indicated treatment and participate as members of the interdisciplinary team to support a vast continuum of outcomes.

Research in music therapy supports the effectiveness of interventions in many areas such as overall physical rehabilitation and facilitating movement, increasing motivation to become engaged in treatment, providing emotional support for clients and their families, and creating an outlet for expression of feelings. Music therapists are employed in many different settings including general hospitals, schools, mental health agencies, rehabilitation centers, nursing homes, forensic settings, and private practice.

Professional Membership

The profession of music therapy has over a 50-year legacy in the United States. The American Music Therapy Association (AMTA) was founded in 1998 as a result of the union of the American Association for Music Therapy (AAMT - founded in 1971) and the National Association for Music Therapy (NAMT - founded in 1950). Its mission is to advance public awareness of the benefits of music therapy and to increase access to quality music therapy services. AMTA is committed to the advancement of education, training, professional standards, and research in support of the music therapy profession.

Professional members of AMTA hold bachelor's degrees or higher in music therapy from accredited colleges or universities. The credential 'MT-BC" (Music Therapist-Board Certified) is issued by the Certification Board for Music Therapists (CBMT), an independent, non-profit corporation fully accredited by the National Commission for Certifying Agencies. The "MT-BC" is granted by the CBMT upon successful completion of 1) an AMTA approved academic and clinical training program and 2) a written objective national examination.

Prior to 1998, those individuals who successfully completed the rigorous degree requirements of an NAMT or AAMT approved program and internship were issued the designations of Registered Music Therapist (RMT), Certified Music Therapist (CMT), or Advanced Certified Music Therapist (ACMT). The National Music Therapy Registry maintains a listing of current RMTs, CMTs, and ACMTs.

8455 COLESVILLE ROAD

SUITE 1000

SILVER SPRING, MD 20910

PHONE (301) 589 - 3300

FAX (301) 589 - 5175

E-MAIL INFO@MUSICTHERAPY.ORG

Quality Assurance

AMTA provides several mechanisms for monitoring the quality of music therapy programs. These include: established criteria for the education and clinical training of music therapists, Standards of Practice, Professional Competencies, Code of Ethics, Peer Review system, a Judicial Review Board and an Ethics Board.

Governing Bodies

AMTA is governed by a 15-member Board of Directors, which consists of both elected and appointed officers. Board meetings are held 2-3 times each year. Policies are set by an Assembly of Delegates consisting of representatives from each of the Association's eight regional chapters. Thirteen standing committees represent the areas of: Academic Program Approval, Association Internship Approval, Government Relations, Membership, Reimbursement, Research, Standards of Clinical Practice, Special Target Populations, Professional Advocacy, Employment/Public Relations, Continuing Education, International Relations, Affiliate Relations, along with an Education and Training Advisory Board.

Publications and Technical Resources

- *Journal of Music Therapy* – a quarterly research-oriented journal
- *Music Therapy Perspectives* – a semi-annual, practice-oriented journal
- *Music Therapy Matters* – a quarterly newsletter
- *Member Sourcebook* – annual directory and statistical profile of AMTA membership
- www.musictherapy.org - access to up-to-date information
- Conference Programs, Monographs, Bibliographies, Videos, Fact Sheets, Brochures
- Advocacy assistance for consumers, families, educators and healthcare professionals
- Practice support to music therapy clinicians, students and professors

Continuing Education

AMTA holds an annual meeting every fall, offering concurrent sessions, pre-conference institutes, and intensive courses for members' professional development. Each of the 8 AMTA regions also holds a conference in the spring of each year, providing additional opportunities for continuing education. Several other workshops and symposiums are available throughout the year to help meet members' educational and clinical needs.

Affiliations

NCCATA	The National Coalition of Creative Arts Therapies Associations
JCAHO	Joint Commission on Accreditation of Healthcare Organizations
CARF	The Rehabilitation Accreditation Commission
CCD	Consortium for Citizens with Disabilities
NAPSO	National Alliance of Pupil Services Organizations
HPN	Health Professions Network
NRC	National Rehabilitation Caucus
CMS – NMEP	Centers for Medicare and Medicaid Services National Medicare Education Program Partner

MUSIC THERAPY REIMBURSEMENT FACTS

AMERICAN
MUSIC
THERAPY
ASSOCIATION

Medicare

Since 1994, music therapy has been identified as a reimbursable service under benefits for Partial Hospitalization Programs (PHP). Falling under the heading of Activity Therapy, the interventions cannot be purely recreational or diversionary in nature and must be individualized and based on goals specified in the treatment plan. The current HCPCS Code for PHP is G0176.

The music therapy must be considered an *active treatment* by meeting the following criteria:

1) Be prescribed by a physician;
2) Be reasonable and necessary for the treatment of the individual's illness or injury;
3) Be goal directed and based on a documented treatment plan;
4) The goal of treatment cannot be to merely maintain current level of functioning; the individual must exhibit some level of improvement.

Medicaid

As Medicaid programs vary from state-to-state, so do the Medicaid coverage avenues for music therapy services. Some private practice music therapists have successfully applied for Medicaid provider numbers within their states. Some states offer waiver programs in which music therapy can be covered. In some situations, although music therapy is not specifically listed as a covered service, due to functional outcomes achieved, music therapy interventions can fall under an existing treatment category such as community support, rehabilitation, or habilitation.

Examples

Arizona—Medicaid coverage for music therapy provided to individuals with developmental disabilities; originally recognized as a habilitation service but also considered as a socialization service.

Minnesota—Individual music therapist received provider number to service clients with mental illness and developmental disabilities. Waiver program for children with developmental disabilities provides coverage for music therapy.

Pennsylvania—Department of Aging Waiver program allows Medicaid payment for music therapy provided in a community based setting. Music therapy is listed under health and mental health related counseling services.

8455 COLESVILLE ROAD

SUITE 1000

SILVER SPRING, MD 20910

PHONE (301) 589 - 3300

FAX (301) 589 - 5175

E-MAIL INFO@MUSICTHERAPY.ORG

North Carolina—Medicaid reimbursement is available for music therapy services through the Community Alternatives Program (CAP) for clients with developmental disabilities.

Indiana—Waiver program for children with developmental disabilities offers coverage for music therapy.

Michigan—Music therapy is a covered service under the state's Medicaid Children's Waiver Program.

Private Insurance

- The number of success stories involving third party reimbursement for the provision of music therapy services continues to grow. Over the past twelve years a growing public demand for music therapy services has been accompanied by a demand for third party reimbursement. In response to the increasing demand the music therapy profession has worked to facilitate the reimbursement process for clients of music therapy services.
- The American Music Therapy Association now estimates that at least 20% of music therapists receive third party reimbursement for the services they provide. This number is expected to increase exponentially as music therapy occupies a strong position in the health care industry.
- Insurance companies are recognizing the advantages of including music therapy as a benefit as they respond to the increasing market demand for greater patient choice of health care services. Companies like, Blue Cross/Blue Shield, Humana, Great West Life, Aetna, Metropolitan, and Provident have reimbursed for music therapy services on a case-by-case basis, based on medical necessity.
- Music therapy is comparable to other health professions like occupational therapy and physical therapy in that individual assessments are provided for each client, service must be found reasonable and necessary for the individual's illness or injury and interventions include a goal-directed documented treatment plan.
- Like other therapies, music therapy is typically pre-approved for coverage or reimbursement, and is found to be reimbursable when deemed medically necessary to reach the treatment goals of the individual patient. Therefore, reimbursement for services is determined on a case-by-case basis and is available in a large variety of health care settings, with patients with varying diagnoses.

Other Sources

Additional sources for reimbursement and financing of music therapy services include: many state departments of mental health, state departments of mental retardation/developmental disabilities, state adoption subsidy programs, private auto insurance, employee worker's compensation, county boards of mental retardation/developmental disabilities, IDEA Part B related services funds, foundations, grants, and private pay.

Research Briefs

- Music Therapy in General Medical Settings

- Music Therapy in Behavioral Health

- Music Therapy in the Area of Child Development and Human Growth

- Music Therapy in Neurologic Rehabilitation

- Music Therapy in Senior Adult Populations

- Music Therapy in Oncology

 # American Music Therapy Association, Inc.

8455 Colesville Road, Suite 1000, Silver Spring, MD 20910   (301) 589-3300   fax (301) 589-5175
email: amta@musictherapy.org   website: www.musictherapy.org

Music Therapy in General Medical Settings

Overview of Typical Services for this Population:

Music therapy services for adults and children may take place in inpatient and outpatient medical settings. Music therapists develop a therapeutic relationship with their patients and use music and the relationship to maintain, restore or improve mental and physical health. With medical patients, treatment goals tend to focus upon: 1) reduction of anxiety, depression and pain, 2) improvements in cardiac and pulmonary function, mobility, and mood; 3) weight gain, developmental growth, and attachment with caregivers for premature infants; and 4) improvements in immune functions. Outcomes appear to be mediated through the subject's emotional, cognitive and interpersonal responsiveness to the music and/or the supportive music therapy relationship. The following citations are examples of current research.

Annotated Bibliography of Research: 1992–2003

- **Reviews of Music Therapy in medical settings.**

  Standley, J. M. (2000). Music research in medical treatment. In American Music Therapy Association (Ed.), *Effectiveness of music therapy procedures: Documentation of research and clinical practice* (3rd ed.; pp. 1–64). Silver Spring, MD: American Music Therapy Association.

  Standley, J. M. (1992). Meta analysis of research in music and medical treatment. Effect size as a basis for comparisons across multiple dependent and independent variables. In R. Spintge & R. Droh (Eds.), *Music Medicine* (pp. 364–378). St Louis, MO: MMB.

- **Music Therapy promotes stimulation of calm, alert awake state for premature infants.**

  Courtnage, A., Chawla, H., Loewy, J., & Nolan, P. (2002). Effects of live infant directed singing on oxygen saturation, heart rate and respiratory rates of infants in the neonatal intensive care unit. *Pediatric Research. 51*(4).

  Standley, J. M. (2002). A meta-analysis of the efficacy of music therapy for premature infants. *Journal of Pediatric Nursing, 17*(2), 107–113.

- **Music therapy reduces physiological indicators of anxiety and reduces need for sedation and analgesia, increases completion rate, and shortens examination time during colonoscopy.**

  Schiemann, U., Gross, M., Reuter, R., & Kellner, H. (2002). Improved procedure of colonoscopy under accompanying music therapy. *European Journal of Medical Research. 7*(3), 131–134.

  Smolon, D., Topp, R., & Singer, L. (2002). The effect of self-selected music during colonoscopy on anxiety, heart, rate, and blood pressure. *Applied Nursing Research. 15*(3), 126–136.

- **Music Therapy reduces physiological indicators of pre-operative stress.**

  Miluk-Kolasa, B., Matejek, M., & Stupnicki, R. (1996). The effects of music listening on changes in selected physiological parameters in adult pre-surgical patients. *Journal of Music Therapy, 33*, 208–218.

  Robb, S. L., Nichols R. J., Rutan R. L., & Bishop B. L. (1995). The effects of music assisted relaxation on preoperative anxiety. *Journal of Music Therapy, 32*, 2–21.

- **Music Therapy reduces cortisol in healthy adults.**

  McKinney, C. H., Antoni, M. H., Kumar, M., Tims, F. C., & McCabe, P. M. (1997). Effects of Guided Imagery and Music (GIM) Therapy on mood and cortisol in healthy adults. *Health Psychology 16*(4), 390–400.

- **Music Therapy reduces physiological and psychological indicators of distress in post-operative cardiac patients.**

  Cadigan, M. E., Caruso, N. A., Halderman, S. M., McNamara, M. E., Noyes, D. A., Spadafora, M. A., & Carrol, D. L. (2001). The effect of music on cardiac patients on bed rest. *Progress in Cardiovascular Nursing, 16*(1), 5–13.

- **Music Therapy has potential to produce cumulative or sustaining neuroendocrine or immunological effects contributing to well–being.**

  Bittman, B. B., Berk, L. S., Felten, D. L., Westengard, J., Simonton, O. C., Pappas, J., & Ninehouser, M. (2001). Composite effects of group drumming music therapy on modulation of neuroendocrine-immune parameters in normal subjects. *Alternative Therapies in Health & Medicine, 7*(1), 38–47.

  Hasegawa, Y., Kubota, N., Unagaki, T., & Shinagawa, N. (2001). Music therapy induced alterations in natural killer cell count and function. *Japanese Journal of Geriatrics. 38*(2), 201–204.

- **Music Therapy reduces pain.**

  Fratianne, R. B, Presner, J. D., Houston, M. J., Super, D. M., Yowler, C. J., & Standley, J. M. (2001). The effect of music-based imagery and musical alternate engagement on the burn debridement process. *Journal of Burn Care & Rehabilitation, 22*(1), 47–53.

  Good, M., Anderson, G. C., Stanton-Hicks, M., Grass, J. A., & Makil, M. (2002). Relaxation and music reduce pain after gynecologic surgery. *Pain Management Nursing, 3*(2), 61–70.

This information was excerpted from a paper that was prepared by Paul Nolan, M.C.A.T., MT-BC, LPC, Drexel University's Hahnemann Creative Arts in Therapy Program for the Mid-Atlantic Region of the American Music Therapy Association for the National Institutes of Health, "Music and Medicine Symposium" on March 20, 2003.

American Music Therapy Association, Inc.

8455 Colesville Road, Suite 1000, Silver Spring, MD 20910   (301) 589-3300   fax (301) 589-5175
email: amta@musictherapy.org   website: www.musictherapy.org

Music Therapy in Behavioral Health

Overview of Typical Services with this Population:

Music therapists serve persons having personal issues in a variety of settings including public and private psychiatric hospitals or schools, mental health centers, correctional and forensic facilities, and substance abuse treatment programs. Music therapists use music to enhance social or interpersonal, affective, cognitive, and behavioral functioning. Research indicates music therapy is effective at reducing muscle tension, anxiety, and at promoting relaxation, verbalization, interpersonal relationships, and group cohesiveness. This can set the stage for open communication and provide a starting place for a non-threatening discussion of personal issues. A therapist can talk with a client, but music can link the dialogue to their feelings.

Annotated Bibliography of Research: 1993–2003

I. Music therapy research with adolescents and children.

- Depressed adolescents listening to music experienced a significant decrease in stress hormone (cortisol) levels, and most adolescents shifted toward left frontal EEG activation (associated with positive affect).

   Field, T., Martinez, A., Nawrocki, T., Pickens, J., Fox N. A., & Schanberg, S. (1998). Music shifts frontal EEG in depressed adolescents. *Adolescence, 33*(129), 109–116.

- Music therapy clients significantly improved on the Aggression/Hostility scale of Achenbach's Teacher's Report Form, suggesting that group music therapy can facilitate self-expression and provide a channel for transforming frustration, anger, and aggression into the experience of creativity and self-mastery.

   Montello, L. M., & Coons, E. E. (1998). Effect of active versus passive group music therapy on preadolescents with emotional, learning, and behavioral disorders. *Journal of Music Therapy, 35,* 49–67.

II. Music therapy research with adults.

- One month of music therapy sessions significantly diminished patients' negative symptoms, increased their ability to converse with others, reduced their social isolation, and increased their level of interest in external events.

   Tang, W., Xinwei, Y., & Zhanpei, Z. (1994). Rehabilitative effect of music therapy for residual schizophrenia: A one-month randomized controlled trial in Shanghai. *British Journal of Psychiatry, 165* (Supp. 24), 38–44.

- Patients with schizophrenia at the end of 10 music therapy sessions showed significant improvement of the Brief Psychiatric Rating Scale and increased their level of musical interaction with the therapist.

  Pavlicevic, M., Trevarthen, C., & Duncan, J. (1994). Improvisational music therapy and the rehabilitation of persons suffering from chronic schizophrenia. *Journal of Music Therapy, 31*(2), 86–104.

- The anxiety level of psychiatric inpatients was significantly reduced using progressive muscle relaxation, meditative breathing, guided imagery and soft music to promote relaxation.

  Weber, S. (1996, September). The effects of relaxation exercises on anxiety levels in psychiatric inpatients. *Journal of Holistic Nursing, 14*(3), 196–205.

III. Research on affective meaning in music.

- The accuracy of identifying the emotional content in music partially depends upon the emotion expressed and the instrument used to perform the music.

  Behrens, G. A. (1997). *A psychometric evaluation of the MPEC-A measure to assess accuracy in identifying emotions represented by music improvisations.* Unpublished doctoral dissertation, University of Kansas.

  Behrens, G. A., & Green, S. B. (1993). The ability to identify emotional content of solo improvisations performed vocally and on three different instruments. *Psychology of Music, 21*, 20–33.

- The more similar music components are (which are used to express different emotions), the more difficult it is to identify the emotions expressed.

  Behrens, G. A. (1997). *A psychometric evaluation of the MPEC-A measure to assess accuracy in identifying emotions represented by music improvisations.* Unpublished doctoral dissertation, University of Kansas.

This information was excerpted from a paper that was prepared by Michael D. Cassity, Ph.D., MT-BC, Drury University, for the Mid-Atlantic Region of the American Music Therapy Association for the National Institutes of Health, "Music and Medicine Symposium" on March 20, 2003.

American Music Therapy Association, Inc.

8455 Colesville Road, Suite 1000, Silver Spring, MD 20910   (301) 589-3300   fax (301) 589-5175
email: amta@musictherapy.org   website: www.musictherapy.org

Music Therapy in the Area of Child Development and Human Growth

Overview of Typical Services with this Population:

Young children receive music therapy across a wide range of settings: in an educational IEP as a related service for a specific objective, in early intervention programs as an integral part of the curriculum, or in hospital settings such as the NICU or Pediatric ICU. Music activities are provided in an intentional and developmentally appropriate format to enhance verbal, social/emotional, sensorimotor, and/or cognitive skills. Music is multi-modal, stimulating multiple senses and activating different areas of the brain. It is highly motivating for young children and encourages socialization, communication, and motor development. It also masks the perception of pain and trauma and helps reduce developmental regression of hospitalized young children.

Annotated Bibliography of Research: 1993–2003

I. **Music Therapy Research with Premature Infants**

- Music listening increases oxygen saturation.

    Cassidy, J. W., & Standley, J. M. (1995). The effect of music listening on physiological responses of premature infants in the NICU. *Journal of Music Therapy, 32*(4), 208–227.

    Standley, J. M., & Moore, R. S. (1995). Therapeutic effects of music and mother's voice on premature infants. *Pediatric Nursing, 21*(6), 509–512.

- Music increases tolerance for stimulation and results in earlier discharge.

    Standley, J. M. (1998). The effect of music and multimodal stimulation on responses of premature infants in neonatal intensive care. *Pediatric Nursing, 24*(6), 532–539.

- Premature infants are reinforced by music, discriminate the contingent relationship within 2.5 minutes, and significantly increase sucking rate.

    Standley, J. M. (2000). The effect of contingent music to increase non-nutritive sucking of premature infants. *Pediatric Nursing, 26*(5), 493–495, 498–499.

- Music reinforced non-nutritive sucking improves feeding rate.

    Standley, J. M. (in press). The effect of music-reinforced non-nutritive sucking on feeding rate of premature infants. *Journal of Pediatric Nursing.*

- A meta-analysis of 10 studies using music in the NICU reveals all results in a positive direction with a mean $d = .83$.

    Standley, J. M. (2002). A meta-analysis of the efficacy of music therapy for premature infants. *Journal of Pediatric Nursing, 17*(2), 107–113.

II.   Music Therapy Research in Infant Learning

- A meta-analysis of 8 studies revealed an overall $d = 1.15$ when music is used to reinforce infant behavior.

   Standley, J. M. (2001, Spring). The power of contingent music for infant learning. *Bulletin of the Council for Research in Music Education, 149,* 65–71.

III.   Music Therapy Research in Pre-Reading/Writing Skill Development

- Music activities increase pre-reading/writing skills, vocabulary development and motor skills in early intervention programs.

   Colwell, C. (1994). Therapeutic application of music in the whole language kindergarten. *Journal of Music Therapy, 31*(4), 238–247.

   Register, D. (2001). The effects of an early intervention music curriculum on prereading/writing. *Journal of Music Therapy, 38*(3), 239–248.

   Standley, J. M., & Hughes, J. E. (1996). Documenting developmentally appropriate objectives and benefits of a music therapy program for early intervention: A behavioral analysis. *Music Therapy Perspectives, 14*(2), 87–94.

   Standley, J. M., & Hughes, J. E. (1997). Evaluation of an early intervention music curriculum for prereading/writing skills. *Music Therapy Perspectives, 15*(2),79–86.

IV.   Music Therapy Rsearch in Cognitive Development

- Music facilitates memory and recall skills of preschoolers.

   Wolfe, D., & Horn, C. (1993). Use of melodies as structural prompts for learning and retention of sequential verbal information by preschool students. *Journal of Music Therapy, 30*(2), 100–118.

   Wolfe, D., & Jellison, J. (1995). Interviews with preschool children about music videos. *Journal of Music Therapy, 25*(2), 265–285.

This information was excerpted from a paper that was prepared by Jayne M. Standley, Ph.D., MT-BC, The Florida State University, for the Mid-Atlantic Region of the American Music Therapy Association for the National Institutes of Health, "Music and Medicine Symposium" on March 20, 2003.

American Music Therapy Association, Inc.

8455 Colesville Road, Suite 1000, Silver Spring, MD 20910   (301) 589-3300   fax (301) 589-5175
email: amta@musictherapy.org   website: www.musictherapy.org

Music Therapy in Neurologic Rehabilitation

Overview of Typical Services with this Population:

Individuals with neurologic disorders receive music therapy across a wide range of settings: in inpatient hospital settings, in outpatient hospital and rehabilitation clinic settings, and in both residential nursing and non-residential day treatment facilities. Therapeutic music interventions are provided to directly enhance motor, cognitive, verbal, and/or social/emotional functioning. The perception of temporal, force, and spatial aspects inherent in music, has been shown to shape subsequent brain and behavior functioning in a therapeutically meaningful manner. Music, specifically rhythm, has been shown to have a significant effect on the central nervous system (CNS) and current research and evidence-based clinical practice provide outcomes which reflect the therapeutic significance of this effect. It is highly motivating for patients of all ages and maintains or increases compliance with treatment protocols.

Annotated Bibliography of Research: 1997–2003

I. Musical Response Models

- Neurological, Physiological, and Psychological Foundations of Musical Behavior.

  Platel, H., Price, C., Baron, J. C., Wise, R., Lambert, J., Frackowiak, R. S. J., Lechevalier, B., & Eustache, R. (1997). The structural components of music perception: A functional anatomical study. *Brain, 120,* 229–243.

  Thaut, M. H., Miller, R. A., & Schauer, L. M. (1998). Multiple synchronization strategies in rhythmic sensorimotor tasks: phase versus period adaptation. *Biological Cybernetics, 79,* 241–250.

  Thaut, M. H., & Petersen, D. A. (2002). Plasticity of neural representations in auditory memory for rhythmic tempo: Trial dependent EEGF spectra. *Proceedings of the Society for Neuroscience,* 373.8.

  Thaut, M. H., & Schauer, M. L. (1997). Weakly coupled oscillators in rhythmic motor synchronization. *Proceedings of the Society for Neuroscience,* 298.20.

II. Mediating Models

- Influence of Music on Non-Musical Behavior.

  Roth, E. A. The effects of music on a language-based analytical task. *Music Perception.* (In review.)

  Thaut, M. H., Rathbun, J., & Miller, R. A. (1997). Music versus metronome timekeeper in a rhythmic motor task. *International Journal of Arts Medicine, 5,* 4–12.

III. Clinical Research Models

- ■ Influence of Auditory Rhythm on Motor and Speech Rehabilitation.

Hurt, C. P., Rice, R. R., McIntosh, G. C., & Thaut, M. H. (1998). Rhythmic auditory stimulation in gait training for patients with traumatic brain injury. *Journal of Music Therapy, 35,* 228–241.

Thaut, M. H., Kenyon, G. P., Hurt, C. P., McIntosh, G. C., & Hoemberg, V. (2002). Kinematic optimization of spatiotemporal patterns in paretic arm training with stroke patients. *Neuropsychologia, 40,* 1073–1081.

Thaut, M. H., McIntosh, G. C., McIntosh, K. W., & Hoemberg, V. (2001). Auditory rhythmicity enhances movement and speech motor control in patients with Parkinson's disease. *Functional Neurology, 16,* 163–172.

Thaut, M. H., Miltner, R., Lange, H. L., Hurt, C. P., & Hoemberg, V. (1999). Velocity modulation and rhythmic synchronization of gait in patients with Huntington's disease. *Movement Disorders, 14,* 808–819.

Thaut, M. H., Schicks, W., McIntosh, G. C., & Hoemberg, V. (in press). The role of motor imagery and temporal cueing in hemiparetic arm rehabilitation. *Journal of Neural Recovery and Repair.*

This information was excerpted from a paper that was prepared by Edward A. Roth, M.M. NMT, MT-BC, Western Michigan University, for the Mid-Atlantic Region of the American Music Therapy Association for the National Institutes of Health, "Music and Medicine Symposium" on March 20, 2003.

American Music Therapy Association, Inc.

8455 Colesville Road, Suite 1000, Silver Spring, MD 20910   (301) 589-3300   fax (301) 589-5175
email: amta@musictherapy.org   website: www.musictherapy.org

Music Therapy in Senior Adult Populations

Overview of Typical Services with this Population:

Music therapists serve a diverse population of senior adults in a variety of settings such as adult day care centers, nursing homes, assisted living facilities, geriatric psychiatric units and VA hospitals. Older adults receiving music therapy services range from independent, "well elderly" individuals to those who have physically disabling conditions or are in the final stages of Alzheimer's Disease. Music therapists use the flexibility inherent in music to design specific activities, which allow the older adult at any level of functioning to experience success, thus promoting a positive quality of life. The pleasant associations, structure and predictability of music offer stability and security, which encourage creative expression and interaction with others. Goals for music therapy intervention are individualized, and may include the use of music to: promote physical exercise, rehabilitation or relaxation; improve cognitive abilities such as attention, concentration and memory; facilitate emotional expression; reduce depression, and enhance spiritual values and the life review process.

Annotated Bibliography of Research: 1993–2003

I. Research on Aging and General Music Abilities

- Aging affects explicit but not implicit memory for melodic material.

  Gaudreau, D. and Peretz, I. (1999). Implicit and explicit memory for music in old and young adults. *Brain and Cognition, 40,* 126–129.

II. Music Therapy Research and Quality of Life

- Participation in organized music activities improves social interaction, well-being and a sense of accomplishment among community-dwelling senior adults.

  Coffman, D. D., & Adamek, M. S. (1999). The contributions of wind band participation to quality of life of senior adults. *Music Therapy Perspectives, 17,* 27–31.

III. Music Therapy Research in Alzheimer's Disease and Related Dementias (ADRD)

- Music experiences can be structured to enhance social/emotional skills, to assist in recall and language skills and to decrease problem behaviors.

  Brotons, M., Koger, S. M., & Pickett-Cooper, P. K. (1997). Music and dementias: A review of literature. *Journal of Music Therapy, 34*(4), 204–245.

- A meta-analysis of 21 studies using music in ADRD yielded an effect size $d = .7879$ indicating that music significantly reduces symptoms associated with ADRD.

  Koger, S. M., Chapin, K., & Brotons, M. (1999). Is music therapy an effective intervention for dementia? A meta-analytic review of literature. *Journal of Music Therapy, 36*(1), 2–15.

- Music is effective in decreasing the frequency of agitated and aggressive behaviors.

  Brotons, M., & Pickett-Cooper, P. K. (1996). The effects of music therapy intervention on agitation behaviors of Alzheimer's disease patients. *Journal of Music Therapy, 33*(1), 2–18.

  Clark, M. E., Lipe, A. W., & Bilbrey, M. (1998). Use of music to decrease aggressive behaviors in people with dementia. *Journal of Gerontological Nursing, 24*(7), 10–17.

  Groene, R. W. (1993). Effectiveness of music therapy 1:1 intervention with individuals having senile dementia of the Alzheimer's type. *Journal of Music Therapy, 30*(3), 138–157.

- Individuals in the late stages of dementia respond to and interact with music.

  Clair, A. A. (1996). The effect of singing on alert responses in persons with late stage dementia. *Journal of Music Therapy, 33*(4), 234–247.

IV. Psychometric Research in Music Therapy and ADRD

- Music tasks can be used to assess cognitive ability in people with ADRD.

  Lipe, A. (1995). The use of music performance tasks in the assessment of cognitive functioning among older adults with dementia. *Journal of Music Therapy, 32*(3), 137–151.

- Residual music skills can be measured in ways that are both reliable and valid.

  York, E. F. (2000). A test-retest reliability study of the Residual Music Skills Test. *Psychology of Music, 28,* 174–180.

  York, E. F. (1994). The development of a quantitative music skills test for patients with Alzheimer's disease. *Journal of Music Therapy, 31*(4), 280–296.

This information was excerpted from a paper that was prepared by Anne Lipe, Ph.D., MT-BC, Shenandoah University, for the Mid-Atlantic Region of the American Music Therapy Association for the National Institutes of Health, "Music and Medicine Symposium" on March 20, 2003.

American Music Therapy Association, Inc.

8455 Colesville Road, Suite 1000, Silver Spring, MD 20910   (301) 589-3300   fax (301) 589-5175
email: amta@musictherapy.org   website: www.musictherapy.org

Music Therapy in Oncology

Overview of Typical Services with this Population:

Music therapy has been utilized with both children and adults in oncology settings for treating psychological and physical issues associated both with the disease process and with its treatment. Participating in music therapy reduces anxiety, elevates mood, decreases pain, reduces nausea and emesis, and enhances quality of life. While recorded music is more beneficial than no-music conditions, live music is most beneficial with this population. Among pediatric oncology patients, music decreases anxiety, encourages engaging behaviors, and reduces distress during medical procedures. In a medical meta-analysis, Standley (2000) analyzed 18 experimental studies and determined an overall Effect Size of .57 for cancer patients receiving music therapy.

> Standley, J. M. (2000). Music research in medical treatment. In AMTA (Ed.), *Effectiveness of Music Therapy Procedures: Documentation of Research and Clinical Practice* (3rd ed.). Silver Spring, MD: American Music Therapy Association.

Annotated Bibliography of Music Therapy in Oncology: 1991–2003

I.   Music Therapy Research in Adult Oncology: Psychological Issues

- Engaging in group music therapy and listening to music reduces anxiety associated with chemotherapy and radiotherapy.

  > Cai, G., Qiao, Y., Li, P., & Lu, L. (2001). Music therapy in treatment of cancer patients. *Chinese Mental Health Journal, 15*(3), 179–181.

  > Harper, E. I. (2001). *Reducing treatment-related anxiety in cancer patients: Comparison of psychological interventions.* Unpublished doctoral dissertation: Southern Methodist University.

  > Sabo, C. E., & Michael, S. R. (1996). The influence of personal message with music on anxiety and side effects associated with chemotherapy. *Cancer Nursing, 19*(4), 283–289.

- Responding to and engaging in music-making experiences increases mood state scores of cancer patients as does participation in Guided Imagery and Music sessions.

  > Burns, D. S. (2001). The effect of the bonny method of guided imagery and music on the mood and life quality of cancer patients. *Journal of Music Therapy, 38*(1), 51–65.

  > Waldon, E. G. (2001). The effects of group music therapy on mood states and cohesiveness in adult oncology patients. *Journal of Music Therapy, 38*(3), 212–238.

- Participating in cognitive-behavioral music therapy sessions, guided imagery and music, and inner image relaxation increases the quality of life of cancer patients.

  Burns, D. S. (2001). The effect of the Bonny Method of Guided Imagery and Music on the mood and life quality of cancer patients. *Journal of Music Therapy, 38*(1), 51–65.

  Hilliard, R. E. (2003). The effects of music therapy on the quality and length of life of people diagnosed with terminal cancer. *Journal of Music Therapy, 40*(2), 113–137.

  Xie, Z., Wang, G., Yin, Z., Liao, S., Lin, J., Yu, Z., & Liu, G. (2001). Effect of music therapy and inner image relaxation on quality of life in cancer patients receiving chemotherapy. *Chinese Mental Health Journal, 15*(3), 176–178.

II. Music Therapy in Adult Oncology: Physiological Issues

- Listening to music reduces nausea and emesis for patients receiving chemotherapy.

  Standley, J. M. (1992). Clinical applications of music and chemotherapy: The effects on nausea and emesis. *Music Therapy Perspectives, 10*, 27–35.

- Engaging in music therapy sessions enhances immune functioning among cancer subjects.

  Cai, G., Qiao, Y., Li, P., & Lu, L. (2001). Music therapy in treatment of cancer patients. *Chinese Mental Health Journal, 15*(3), 179–181.

  Nunez, M., et al. (2002). Music, immunity, and cancer. *Life Sciences, 71*(9), 1047–1057.

- Participating in music therapy sessions increases comfort and motivates bone marrow transplant patients during treatment.

  Boldt, S. (1996). The effects of music therapy on motivation, psychological well-being, physical comfort, and exercise endurance of bone marrow transplant patients. *Journal of Music Therapy, 33*, 164–188.

III. Music Therapy in Adult Oncology: Palliative Care and End of Life

- Listening to music alleviates pain, fatigue, and anxiety of hospice cancer patients.

  Longfield, V. (1995). *The effects of music therapy on pain and mood in hospice patients.* Unpublished master's thesis, St. Louis University.

- Engaging in cognitive-behavioral music therapy sessions significantly increases the quality of life of hospice cancer patients.

  Hilliard, R. E. (2003). The effects of music therapy on the quality and length of life of people diagnosed with terminal cancer. *Journal of Music Therapy, 40*(2), 113–137.

IV. Music Therapy in Pediatric Oncology

- Participating in live music therapy sessions enhances immune functioning of pediatric oncology patients.

  Lane, D. (1991). The effect of a single music therapy session on hospitalized children as measured by salivary Immunoglobulin A, speech pause time, and a patient opinion Likert scale. *Pediatric Research, 29*(4), 11A.

- Music therapy serves to decrease behavioral distress among pediatric oncology patients during needle sticks.

  Malone, A. B. (1996). The effects of live music on the distress of pediatric patients receiving intravenous starts, venipunctures, injections, and heel sticks. *Journal of Music Therapy, 33*(1), 19–33.

- Music provides an environment for engaging behaviors and decreasing distress behaviors for isolated pediatric oncology patients.

  Robb, S. L. (2000). The effect of therapeutic music interventions on the behavior of hospitalized children in isolation: developing a contextual support model of music therapy. *Journal of Music Therapy, 37*(2), 118–146.

This information was excerpted from a paper that was prepared by Russell E. Hilliard, Ph.D., LCSW, MT-BC, State University of New York at New Paltz, for the Mid-Atlantic Region of the American Music Therapy Association for the National Institutes of Health, "Music and Medicine Symposium" on March 20, 2003.

Conclusion

All music therapists need to understand the basics of third-party reimbursement for music therapy services. Even though some individuals are employed full-time in facilities that cover music therapy expenses through "per-diem" rates and perhaps even under the Medicare PPS system, it is good business to know how healthcare is funded. More and more clinicians are being presented with opportunities to seek coverage from private insurance, Medicaid, waiver programs, and other state funding sources. In order to navigate these payment options successfully, clinicians must become acquainted with their structure.

The good news is, if you are reading this section after having read the preceding pages, you are well on your way to having the knowledge necessary for reimbursement success. It is important to remember that you will not know if you can receive third-party payments until you try! The music therapists who have achieved this goal did not wait for someone else to call the insurance company or for someone else to fill out the paperwork. The music therapists who report the most reimbursement success are those who took the initiative to seek coverage so that a client could receive services. The motivation comes from not just the need to increase access in general, but also the desire to increase access to music therapy for the clients you serve!

It was exciting to review the data from the web-based survey and in-depth telephone interviews of music therapists successfully pursuing and receiving reimbursement. Although AMTA had previously gathered anecdotal information over the years about some of these accomplishments, these recent data provide details that will help to move the association's reimbursement efforts forward. The best practice results not only validated the payment sources we were anticipating, but also highlighted areas of available coverage that warrant further exploration and development.

As professionals approach any new reimbursement opportunity, they might discover the experience similar to implementing music therapy strategies within a new treatment setting. In both situations, it is important to adapt methods and materials to meet the needs of the clients served. Not all reimbursement cases will be handled in the same manner, even if working with the same third-party payer. Keep in mind that each time you apply the techniques outlined in this guide, the process becomes more refined and your professional development skills expand.

Throughout the process, feel confident in your ability as a therapist and as a viable healthcare provider. The music therapy profession is supported by over 50 years of applications in a wide variety of healthcare environments. When advocating for reimbursement, present your assessments and recommended treatment strategies with confidence. Demonstrate how music therapy can address functional outcomes and illustrate goal achievement with supportive research.

When advocating for music therapists as qualified providers, outline the professions required Education, Clinical Training, and Board Certification. Emphasize the importance of adherence to AMTA's Standards of Clinical Practice and Code of Ethics as well as CBMT's Code of Professional Practice. AMTA's history, mission, and structure, along with CBMT's certification/ recertification credentialing program, all contribute to the professional recognition necessary for reimbursement.

In the end, be proud of your skills and knowledge as a music therapist. Assertively "defend" the value of the profession. Understanding the information in this guide, designed to provide best practices and procedures in music therapy reimbursement, is one positive step in the advancement of your clinical practice. Taking the next step to actually implement the recommended procedures and ultimately assist AMTA with its mission of increasing access to quality music therapy services is up to you.

> I can give you a six-word formula for success:
> Think things through—then follow through.
>
> —Edward Rickenbacker

Good luck!

Appendix

AMTA Operational Plan Reimbursement Initiative

Included below are the AMTA Strategic Plan advocacy objective and the operational plan outline for the reimbursement initiative. As you review this information, you will discover the important role each music therapist plays in this plan by increasing his or her own knowledge of the reimbursement process.

STRATEGIC PLAN GOAL II. ADVOCACY. 2.3

Develop strategies that will support the development of legislation, regulations, policies, and programs that will increase access to and funding for music therapy services and programs.

REIMBURSEMENT AND FINANCING PRIMARY GOAL

Increase access to music therapy services by increasing the percentage of music therapy services receiving reimbursement.

PROJECTED OUTCOMES

1. Music therapists have basic knowledge of the process of reimbursement and financing for music therapy services.

2. Insurance companies, both private and public, have the necessary information, education, and training in music therapy benefits and applications in order to make informed decisions about reimbursing music therapy services.

3. Service providers, i.e., physicians, case managers, administrators, healthcare professionals, etc., have the necessary information, education, and training in music therapy benefits and applications in order to make informed decisions about providing music therapy services in facilities, agencies, and institutions.

4. Consumers, i.e., clients, parents, family members, advocates, etc., have the necessary information about music therapy benefits and applications in order to make informed decisions about requesting and/or selecting music therapy services.

OUTCOME 1

Music therapists have basic knowledge of the process of reimbursement and financing for music therapy services.

Objectives and Tasks

I.1. Define and articulate the "basic knowledge" of reimbursement and financing.

    I.1.a. Hire a consultant to assist in researching and defining basic knowledge of reimbursement and financing.

    I.1.b. Convene a blue ribbon panel (multi-discipline) to discuss and synthesize the state-of-the-art and trends in healthcare financing, reacting to the work of the consultant.

    I.1.c. Publish blue ribbon panel report.

I.2. Determine current state of financing of music therapy services, including trends in reimbursement and music therapy successes.

    I.2.a. Conduct in-depth study of profession of music therapy in order to compile detailed case studies of reimbursement and financing successes in music therapy.

    I.2.b. Publish a best practices manual on reimbursement and financing in music therapy utilizing case studies, survey results, and consultant report findings.

    1.2.c. Convene periodic (biennial) blue ribbon panels to conduct state-of-the-art research in healthcare and music therapy financing.

I.3. Recommend the inclusion of basic knowledge of reimbursement and financing of music therapy services in AMTA competencies and AMTA Standards of Clinical Practice.

    I.3.a. Following blue ribbon panel and best practices research, identify necessary competencies for music therapists in reimbursement and financing of music therapy services.

    I.3.b. Given that the process of music therapy practice includes knowledge of how the service is financed, develop and adopt relevant standards for Clinical Practice.

    I.3.c. Consult with CBMT Executive Board and Executive Director regarding reimbursement and financing of music therapy services.

I.4.   Develop competence in reimbursement and financing for undergraduate and graduate music therapy programs, clinicians, and educators.

I.4.a.   Develop teaching strategies and materials for undergraduate and graduate music therapy programs.

I.4.b.   Develop continuing education courses for clinicians and educators. Continuing education opportunities may include national, regional, and state conferences; audio conferences; video/audio/CD-ROM courses; web-based courses.

OUTCOME 2

Insurance companies, both private and public, have the necessary information, education, and training in music therapy benefits and applications in order to make informed decisions about reimbursing music therapy services.

Objectives and Tasks

II.1.   Identify the data and research required by insurance companies to facilitate reimbursement of music therapy services.

II.1.a.   Outline criteria necessary for music therapy research and credentials to meet the requirements of insurance companies.

II.1.b.   Establish research agenda priorities to include research projects demonstrating the efficacy and cost effectiveness of music therapy.

II.2.   Develop an advocacy and marketing plan for educating public and private insurance companies.

II.2.a.   Convene group of insurance advisors and music therapists to identify target audiences and develop materials.

II.2.b.   Determine time line, task list, and method for implementation on national, regional, and local levels.

II.2.c.   Incorporate education of CMS representatives within the national marketing plan.

II.3.   Identify the accepted credential standards in healthcare financing and reimbursement.

II.3.a.   Identify standards and compare with music therapy credential standards.

II.3.b.   Educate AMTA leadership, committees, and membership on industry credential standards and the relationship with music therapy credential standards.

II.4. Communicating with CBMT, develop plan to facilitate the acceptance of MT-BC as the recognized credential for music therapists by state and federal regulatory bodies.

II.4.a. Utilize Assembly-authorized Occupational Regulation Study to assess current status of music therapy credential acceptance.

II.4.b. Communicating with CBMT, develop regional campaign to disseminate credential information to appropriate state agencies and officials, insurance companies, and other music therapy financing sources.

OUTCOME 3

Service providers, i.e., physicians, case managers, administrators, healthcare professionals, etc., have the necessary information, education, and training in music therapy benefits and applications in order to make informed decisions about providing music therapy services in facilities, agencies, and institutions.

Objectives and Tasks

III.1. Develop marketing plan for service providers, including information on financing, standards of clinical practice, code of ethics, and credentials.

III.1.a. Convene group of service providers and music therapists to identify target audiences and develop materials.

III.1.b. Determine time line, task list, and method for implementation on national, regional, and local levels.

OUTCOME 4

Consumers, i.e., clients, parents, family members, advocates, etc., have the necessary information about music therapy benefits and applications in order to make informed decisions about requesting and/or selecting music therapy services.

Objectives and Tasks

IV.1. Develop marketing plan for providing information to consumers, including information on the benefits and applications of music therapy, financing, credentials, and availability.

IV.1.a. Convene group of consumers and music therapists to determine best marketing methods.

IV.1.b. Develop accessible resources for national distribution.

IV.1.c. Provide developed materials to AMTA membership for dissemination on the local level.

References

Alkire, A., et al. (1995). *Managed Care: Integrating the Delivery and Financing of Health Care, Part A*. Washington, DC: The Health Insurance Association of America.

American Heritage® Dictionary of the English Language (4th ed.). (2000). Retrieved October 30, 2003 from http://education.yahoo.com/reference/dictionary/entries/70/ a0107000.html

Blount, L. L., & Waters, J. M. (2001). *Mastering the Reimbursement Process* (3rd ed.). United States: American Medical Association.

Boni, J. A., et al. (2000). *The Health Insurance Primer: An Introduction to How Health Insurance Works*. Washington, DC: The Health Insurance Association of America.

Boudrie, E., et al. (2002). *HCPCS Level II Expert*. United States: Ingenix, Inc.

Care Communications, Inc. *The Record That Defends Its Friends* [Undated pamphlet].

Case Management Society of America. (1996). CMSA Standards of Practice. *Journal of Care Management, 1*(3), 7–16.

Centers for Medicare and Medicaid Services. (2003). *Health Insurance Portability and Accountability Act (HIPAA)—Administrative Simplification*. Retrieved October 22, 2003, from http://www.cms.hhs.gov/hipaa/hipaa2/default.asp

Centers for Medicare and Medicaid Services. (2003). *MDS 2.0 Manuals and Forms*. Retrieved October 7, 2003, from http://www.cms.hhs.gov/Medicaid/mds20/man-form.asp

Centers for Medicare and Medicaid Services. (2003). *Medicare Benefit Policy Manual*. Retrieved November 10, 2003, from http://www.cms.hhs.gov/manuals/102_policy/bp102c02.pdf

Centers for Medicare and Medicaid Services. (2003, September 12). *Medicare Information Resource*. Retrieved October 7, 2003, from http://www.cms.hhs.gov/medicare/default.asp

Centers for Medicare and Medicaid Services. (2003). *Providers*. Retrieved October 7, 2003, from http://www.cms.hhs.gov/providers/

Centers for Medicare and Medicaid Services. (2003). *Welcome to Medicaid*. Retrieved October 9, 2003 from http://www.cms.hhs.gov/states/default.asp

Current Procedural Terminology (CPT®) 2004 Professional Edition. (2003). Chicago: American Medical Association.

Foster, B. (2000). *Developing and Implementing Restorative Programs Seminar.* Baltimore, MD: Heritage Professional Education, LLC.

Hart, A. C., & Hopkins, C. A. (Eds.). (2003). *ICD-9-CM Expert for Hospitals* (Vol. 1, 2, & 3; 6th ed.). United States: Ingenix, Inc.

Hopkins, J. L., & Casacky, T. (Eds.). (1998). *Managed Care: Integrating the Delivery and Financing of Health Care, Part C.* Washington, DC: The Health Insurance Association of America.

Hubbard, M. W., Glover, K. E., & Hartley, C. P. (2003). *HIPAA Policies and Procedures Desk Reference.* United States: American Medical Association.

Perkins, J., & Somers, S. (2001). *An Advocate's Guide to the Medicaid Program.* Chapel Hill, NC: National Health Law Program.

Petrie, A., et al. (2003). *Insurance Directory.* United States: Ingenix, Inc.

Rosenbaum, S., Kamoie, B., Mauery, D. R., & Walitt, B., (2003). *Medical Necessity in Private Health Plans: Implications for Behavioral Health Care.* Rockville, MD: Center for Mental Health Services, Substance Abuse and Mental Health Services Administration.

Scovel, M. A., & Houghton, B. (Eds.). (1990). *Reimbursement Guide for Music Therapists: Phase One.* Washington, DC: The National Association for Music Therapy.

Stein, J. J. (Ed.). (1996). *Managed Care: Integrating the Delivery and Financing of Health Care, Part B.* Washington, DC: The Health Insurance Association of America.

Stein, J. J. (Ed.). (1997). *Medical Expense Insurance.* Washington, DC: The Health Insurance Association of America.

United States Department of Health and Human Services. (2003). *Medicare & You 2004.* Baltimore, MD: Centers for Medicare and Medicaid Services.

Resources

Music Therapy

American Music Therapy Association
8455 Colesville Road
Suite 1000
Silver Spring, MD 20910
T: 301-589-3300
F: 301-589-5175
www.musictherapy.org

Certification Board for Music Therapists
506 East Lancaster Avenue, Suite 102
Downingtown, PA 19335
T: 800-765-2268
T: 610-269-8900
www.cbmt.com

Medicare and Medicaid

Centers for Medicare and Medicaid Services (CMS)
7500 Security Boulevard
Baltimore, MD 21244-1850
http://www.cms.hhs.gov/

State Medicaid Programs

http://www.cms.hhs.gov/medicaid/statemap.asp

HIPAA

Centers for Medicare and Medicaid Services (CMS): http://www.cms.hhs.gov/hipaa/hipaa2

Department of Health and Human Service (HHS) Office for Civil Rights (OCR): www.hhs.gov/ocr/hipaa

Code Manuals: (HCPCS, CPT®, ICD-9-CM)

Ingenix, Inc.
P.O. Box 27116
Salt Lake City, UT 84127-0116
T: 800-464-3649
F: 801-982-4033
www.IngenixOnline.com

American Medical Association
P.O. Box 930876
Atlanta, GA 31193-0876
T: 800-621-8335
F: 312-464-5600
www.amapress.com

Health Insurance and Health Insurance Education

American Association of Health Plans/Health Insurance Association of America (AAHP/HIAA)
These two associations are currently in the process of merging.

American Association of Health Plans
1129 20th Street, NW
Suite 600
Washington, DC 20036
T: 202-778-3200
F: 202-331-7487
www@aahp.org

Health Insurance Association of America
1201 F Street, NW
Suite 500
Washington, DC 20004-1204
T: 202-824-1600
F: 202-824-1722
www.hiaa.org

Grant Information

The Foundation Center
79 Fifth Avenue/16th Street
New York, NY 10003-3076
T: 212-620-4230 or 800-424-9836
F: 212-807-3677
www.fdncenter.org

The Grantsmanship Center
P.O. Box 17220
Los Angeles, CA 90017
T: 213-482-9860
F: 213-482-9863
http://www.tgci.com/